'Having known Patrick when he 
it is sobering to now read how he
have guessed. It makes me won
who appear to be on top of their
the same way. I hope this book w
step forward to ask for help in time and help those around them to
find right way to help. It is honest, authentic and very practical.'
Nick Jenkins, founder of Moonpig, former *Dragons' Den* 'dragon'
and Chairman of Virtual Stock

'To keep mentally healthy is essential if we are to live life to the full.
No book can provide all the answers, but it can provide us with a
guide to keeping mentally well. This book may help you more than
you realise.'
Sir Terry Waite CBE

'Personal, practical and professional – this readable book demonstrates
ways for us all to take positive actions to reach and sustain brighter
days for our wellbeing and resilience.'
Professor Helen Langton, Vice Chancellor of the University of
Suffolk

'*Brighter Days* epitomises Patrick's ability to be both authentic and
hopeful at the same time. We have been friends for years, and I
have seen at first hand his compassion and his desire to help people
to heal. This book welcomes you on a partnered journey to greater
awareness and to lasting change.'
Will van der Hart, priest, coach, communicator and Co-Director of
The Mind and Soul Foundation

'Patrick's book is so accessible, moving and utterly relatable. It
questions our understanding of key words and responses, like
anger, anxiety, resilience, perfectionism and positive vibes, plus it

offers practical advice and exercises to help guide us through our own experiences of the unpredictable state of our mental health. *Brighter Days* could become a Bible to navigate through all of the twenty-first century's challenges.'
Nina Hossain, newscaster, ITV News

'Post-Covid, at a time when so many of us are struggling to establish a "new normal", *Brighter Days* is a cordial for drooping spirits, and an honest, road-tested guide to more hopeful living.'
Lord Richard Chartres

'Readable, practical, wise and kind. This is a book for our times.'
John Sutherland, author and former Chief Superintendent of the Metropolitan Police

'Patrick's writing couldn't be more timely in a world where what things look like in a picture or a post determines who we are, and how we are feeling. *Brighter Days* stands up to that trend of curating an image, wearing a mask and doing everything you can to show that you're holding it together. It's personally helped me start to be more courageous – not like a soldier on a battlefield or a boxer in the ring, but, as Patrick explains, with the courageousness of a person who allows himself to be vulnerable. That message of vulnerability, honesty and self-acceptance is relevant to all of us, and this book will ultimately make you a more content, happier person. It shows us all that whatever our situation, brighter days are possible.'
Sean Fletcher, journalist and BBC presenter

'Patrick reaches to the core of our humanity in a way that few others do. He is articulate, involved and persuasive on some of the key issues which we, as individuals, as professionals, and as a society, face today. Be prepared to be inspired to be better.'
Gerald Walker, President and CEO, ING Americas

'Patrick has presented a range of mental health issues with sensitivity, deep personal experience and warm compassion, allowing the reader to feel seen and understood in our journey to brighter days. He arms us with realistic, practical and achievable strategies to facilitate the reconnection to self, community and faith. I will not hesitate in my recommendation of this book to clients.'
Dr Donna de Lása, HCPC-registered Clinical Psychologist and ISST-certified Schema Therapist

'Honest, vulnerable and practical. This is how we all need to be around mental health, and Patrick's book will help us to get there. It's brave and courageous.'
Dr Charlie Howard, Consultant Clinical Psychologist

'As a therapist, I often wonder how many of my patients could have had a different journey if their early experiences of mental ill health had been met with support, compassion and understanding. While there are no quick fixes to the stigma and shame which surround mental illness, the *Brighter Days* book is a helpful, friendly and accessible step towards a world where emotional and mental health are understood and accepted.'
Clarie Miles, High-Intensity Cognitive Behavioural Therapist, NHS Talking Therapies

'As a GP, I have repeatedly noted the value of helping my patients understand the nature of mental illness. Patrick's book is a masterclass on that. I often see mental health as an incredibly complex muddle of very different jigsaw pieces. As you read Patrick's book, you'll begin to see how the picture of clear emotional wellbeing can emerge, in his words: "beauty from brokenness", "vulnerability is not a weakness" and "floating with anxiety".

Following my own mental health crisis in 2012, a friend visited and commented that he didn't know what to say, but simply offered

to be there. What a gift that was; better than words. Patrick's book will help you to help others… I love it. Please give a copy to a friend.'
Dr Tim Lyttle, GP and NHS leader, Shropshire

'As an NHS GP, I treated many patients over many years with various mental illnesses. I did not, however, consider the issues from the perspective of everyday mental and emotional wellbeing. Through Kintsugi Hope I have engaged with my not-so-bright side more so than throughout my entire forty-three years of practice! *Brighter Days*, written by Patrick in his inimitable style, brings depth and breadth to the subject, and I wholeheartedly recommend it.'
Dr Stephen J. Warren MBChB MRCGP DCH (retired)

'A gravitating read that takes you on a journey of internal realisation and practical ways forward.'
Mrs Nadine Bernard, CEO Aspiring Heads

'*Brighter Days* is an entirely authentic and practical book. It explores themes that are part of the human experience – anxiety, shame, loneliness, anger and grief – and provides some tools for facing the hardships of life. Patrick Regan is empathetic and compassionate. He shares stories from his own life, gains our trust and draws us in. He invites us to look within ourselves with searing honesty, to face our struggles, accept our imperfections and embrace the possibility of healing.'
Rt Revd Dr Guli Francis-Dehqani, Bishop of Chelmsford

BRIGHTER DAYS

12 steps to strengthening your wellbeing

Published in Great Britain in 2023

Society for Promoting Christian Knowledge
RH101, The Record Hall,
16–16A Baldwins Gardens,
London EC1N 7RJ
www.spck.org.uk

British Library Cataloguing-in-Publication Data
A catalogue record for this book is available from the British Library

ISBN 978–0–281–08787–7
eBook ISBN 978–0–281–08788–4
Audio ISBN: 978–0–281–08789–1

1 3 5 7 9 10 8 6 4 2

Typeset by Fakenham Prepress Solutions, Fakenham, Norfolk NR21 8NL
First printed in Great Britain by Clays Ltd, Bungay, Suffolk, NR35 1ED
Subsequently digitally printed in Great Britain
eBook by Fakenham Prepress Solutions, Fakenham, Norfolk NR21 8NL
Produced on paper from sustainable forests

While writing this book, I lost two precious friends to cancer. Their legacy lives on through their families and the huge amount of kindness they showed to those around them. The ways they have, and continue to, inspire me are woven throughout these pages.

To Jean, thanks for being one of the first people to believe in our vision. I miss you.

To Olu, you were a gentle giant, passionate about mental health for those who felt on the margins. You are loved and missed.

Acknowledgements

Thanks to my family: Diane, Keziah, Daniel, Abigail and Caleb. You will always be my number-one priority in life.

I am constantly indebted to Liza, who makes my life so much easier. You are an amazing person, and I learn so much from you. I couldn't have done this without you.

Special thanks to the team at SPCK, especially Elizabeth Neep, who puts up with my endless emails and is so gracious to me. I respect you so much. Thanks also to Wendy Grisham, Louise Titley, Emily Beater, Rio Summers and Joy Tibbs.

My Kintsugi family, especially Jess and Matt Cooper, whose dedication and kindness to the causes they believe in is very humbling. Noleen Andrews, my executive assistant, for organising my days with such diligence and care. My touring team of Lynette Brooks, Joel Harris, Caitlyn Kelly, Mike Coates and Natasha Petrovic (I'm so proud to be your godfather). The wider Kintsugi team, trustees, ambassadors and group leaders: thanks for all you do. The difference you make to people's lives week in, week out is amazing.

The team at Structure by Design: John Galpin, David Davies, Erinna Donohoe and Emma McEniff. I've loved working with you guys. Eddie Donaldson, for all your support, especially for letting me use the White House for some focused writing time. Jane Smith – thanks so much for your poems. They mean so much to me and lots of others. Tara Cutland Green – your support for me is so appreciated.

A huge thank you to all my friends who so kindly endorsed this book, taking time out of their busy schedules to read it – especially Dr Chi-Chi Obuaya for writing the foreword.

Last, but by no means least, my wider family for all their love and support: Mum, Dad, Becky, John, David, Esther and the Whicker Clan.

Contents

About Patrick Regan OBE and Liza Hoeksma   x

Foreword   xi

Introduction   xiii

1   Honesty   1

2   Anxiety   21

3   Depression   39

4   Shame   57

5   Anger   72

6   Grief and loss   89

7   Perfectionism   101

8   Forgiveness   120

9   Self-acceptance   133

10   Healthy relationships   148

11   Resilience   164

12   Brighter days are possible   180

Notes   185

About Patrick Regan OBE and Liza Hoeksma

Patrick Regan OBE is an activist whose passion is speaking about resilience, courage and wellbeing. He founded two award-winning charities – XLP and, most recently, Kintsugi Hope – in partnership with his wife, Diane. Kintsugi Hope has pioneered Kintsugi Wellbeing Groups all over the UK to help people in the area of their mental health. Patrick is a mental health first aider and a campaigner on issues of social justice, and was awarded an OBE for his services to the young by Her Late Majesty Queen Elizabeth II. He is an Honorary Fellow of the South Bank University for his contribution to Justice and Wellbeing. This is Patrick's seventh book. His previous titles cover his work with tackling poverty and educational failure, and his own journey with mental, emotional and spiritual health following major limb reconstruction surgery. Patrick is married to Diane, and they have four children. Find out more on Twitter: @patrickregankh. To book Patrick to speak in your workplace please go to www.brighterdays.life

Liza Hoeksma is a writer who has worked with a number of authors. She has partnered with Patrick Regan on all seven of his books to date. She works in communications for a charity based in Hertfordshire as well as being a life coach, working with clients across the country. Find out more at www.coachingwithliza.com and on Instagram: @Coaching_with_Liza.

Foreword

I first met Patrick at a mutual speaking engagement in 2017. I was struck by the authenticity of his talk and his willingness to make himself vulnerable when discussing his own mental health difficulties and resilience. These were characteristics I encouraged leaders to exhibit in order to build a strong organisational culture in relation to mental health awareness and action. It was encouraging to hear someone walk the walk and, in doing so, give a real sense of hope to others.

I was rushing off to another engagement, but Patrick sought me out, graciously thanked me for my talk and asked me to exchange details with him so that we could connect. I was happy to do so, but was still later struck by the persistence (sadly, my busy diary does not often afford me much flexibility in following up) and intentionality he showed in pursing this opportunity. 'Let's stay in touch' wasn't just a nice sentiment, as is so often the case in these situations; Patrick had the full intention of linking up, and gradually we began collaborating in the mental health and wellbeing space. It has been a privilege to do so with him and to learn from him.

One of Patrick's other great strengths is in providing resources – be it talks, podcasts, webinars or books – for people to better understand and optimise their wellbeing. It has been a privilege to see the two charities he founded have a tangible (rather than simply a theoretical) impact in moving the proverbial mental health and wellbeing needle. XLP has been an exemplar in addressing some of the broader determinants of poor mental health among young people, including poverty, unemployment and family dysfunction. Kintsugi Hope is making real inroads in enabling schools, universities, businesses and churches to become more mental health-friendly, and thus more effective in supporting their congregants living with mental health difficulties.

The timing of this book is incredibly important. On the one hand, coming out of the Covid-19 pandemic I became rather fed up with hearing the cliché 'we live in unprecedented times' thrown into conversations. However, the cliché is true, and I would challenge anyone who says that their resolve has not been tested among the challenges that have been thrown at them in recent years. The pandemic has, on top of other pre-existing factors, left mental health services buckling at the seams and many people struggling to sustain their mental wellbeing, including some who had never experienced mental health difficulties previously or even considered the possibility of struggling in this way.

It has become increasingly apparent to me that the existing structures, personnel and processes cannot adequately meet the society-wide challenge, and we need a broader set of tools we can draw upon, both to become more literate in this area and to harness greater resilience as individuals and communities alike.

I have recommended Patrick's previous books to my patients as a complement to the treatment I provide, and this is another book I will certainly add to the mix. It is a timely, insightful and practical book that will truly make a difference.

Dr Chi-Chi Obuaya, Consultant Psychiatrist

Introduction

There was no time to brake; we were going to hit him. We were returning from a family bowling trip when a car suddenly pulled out in front of us. My dad somehow managed to swerve so that we avoided him, but in doing so we hit a car coming the other way. A 100mph impact. The person who had caused the accident tried to drive off, but my uncle, who was following behind, drove after him and forced him to stop.

I had passed out in the back seat and came round briefly to see that my family were all severely injured. There was blood pouring from my dad's head, and my mum and sister weren't moving. The next thing I was aware of was a nurse hovering above me, asking if I was OK. I got out of the car, shaking and disorientated, desperately looking for my family. I was put in an ambulance with my sister, and we were rushed to the hospital. In A&E I was told my family were all alive, and I ran between them all, trying to check everyone was OK. It was chaotic. Hours later, while my family were admitted to different hospitals, I was sent to stay with my nan. I don't remember crying that night; I think I was in shock and completely bewildered by what had happened. But what I do remember saying to myself is:

Be strong. Hold it together.

No one told me I had to hold it together, certainly no one forced me to, but – as a ten-year-old boy – I took it upon myself regardless. I think it came from a good place. I was motivated by love for my family, wanting to be strong for them. What I've now realised is that, back then, I felt like I was too much – a feeling I have taken forward into my adult life.

For the last thirty years I have founded and grown two charities, and the passion I've felt for the work caused me to push myself hard. I sowed love, sweat and tears into the charities' foundations, desperate to make a difference. As the boss, the buck stops with me, and so I have constantly been aware of the need for income, tried to balance the needs of the staff team and, at times, tried to protect them from difficult decisions that had to be made. Add in being a parent to four kids who naturally have disappointments and challenges of their own, and wanting to be a supportive husband, son, brother and friend, and I have found myself with an overly developed sense of responsibility. This can, in turn, lead to me feeling anxious and exhausted. I know it's impossible to be all things to all people, but the voice inside my head has continued to say:

Be strong. Hold it together.

I know I'm not the only one. Many of us, perhaps especially those of us who have grown up in the UK, have internalised the subliminal and explicit message that we shouldn't show our emotions, that when someone asks how we are, our automatic response should be: 'Fine.' We leave it there – that one word trying to hold all the inevitable highs and lows of life. Now we're learning as a society that *saying* we're fine doesn't actually *make* us fine.

As I've been on this journey, I have discovered some tools to help my wellbeing and that is, in part, what has led to this book; a book about the ups and downs of life; the soul-tearing agonies and the heart-exploding joys. It doesn't offer a set menu – follow these simple steps and all will be well! – but rather, it is intended to help us explore and embrace the messiness of life, acting as a buffet where you can pick and choose what you'd like to dive into next – from understanding anxiety and anger to knowing our true worth and finding our places of true belonging. Because we deserve to be honest about this stuff. The hard things may feel less palatable than the good ones, but they are no less a part of the human experience.

Kintsugi

A number of years ago, in a time of real despair, I came across the Japanese art form of kintsugi. In the UK, if we break a bowl we throw it away or mend it with superglue, hiding the cracks in order to pretend it was never broken. In Japan they put a gold powder in the glue, so instead of hiding the cracks, they make a feature of them. Arguably, the object becomes more beautiful for being broken; it certainty becomes more unique. I believe it is the same in our lives: beauty can come out of brokenness. We can discover treasure in life's scars, and these scars are not things to be ashamed of; they are part of our story. And so, when my wife, Diane, and I wanted to start a new charity to support people with their mental health, and who were experiencing social isolation, 'Kintsugi Hope' was a natural name choice.

Our vision as a charity is to 'see a world where mental and emotional health is understood and accepted with safe and supportive communities for people to grow and flourish'.[1] These are not simply inspirational words. I know first-hand that the times I have flourished were the times when I felt accepted, understood, supported and safe to be myself without judgement, so we wanted to create a practical programme for partner organisations to run in their communities, and online, to help us do just that.

The aim of these groups is to foster an attitude of humility – not to judge, fix or rescue, but to be alongside one another. Groups journey together to learn how to be honest with one another, understand our emotions, build healthy relationships and grow in resilience. Since we started, we have trained thousands of people to become leaders of these groups in their communities, and thousands more have gone through the course in schools, universities, prisons, coffee shops, churches, hairdressers, businesses, sports clubs, community centres and shelters for people experiencing homelessness.

The stories coming back have been beautiful. Some have been dramatic, such as: 'I literally would not be here today if it wasn't for my Kintsugi group; it saved my life,' and, 'This course saved my marriage.' Others came onto the programme feeling overwhelmed and said it gave them the tools to cope with what life threw at them. The latter type of comment is a beautiful reminder that we don't need to be at crisis point before we invest in our mental health. Rather than going to a physio when we've damaged a muscle, it's like going to a gym and building up that muscle to avoid injury in the first place.

The material covered through the Kintsugi Hope courses has been so impactful that we wanted to make these thoughts and teachings accessible to as many people as possible through the book you are holding in your hands. And although a book is no replacement for real community, we do hope that in reading the following pages you are left feeling a little less alone.

Please note: some names have been changed to protect people's identities.

Our humanness

We often talk in terms of our emotional, mental, behavioural and physical health. And yet, spiritual wellbeing is often overlooked, even though the Royal College of Psychiatrists,[2] academics, researchers, GPs and many mental health professionals all agree it has an important part to play in general conversations about health, and particuarly our mental health.

The Mental Health Foundation uses researcher John Swinton's definition of spirituality:

> Spirituality is that aspect of human existence that gives it its 'humanness'. It concerns the structures of significance that give meaning and direction to a person's life and helps them deal with the vicissitudes of existence. As such it includes such vital dimensions as the quest for meaning, purpose, self-transcending knowledge, meaningful relationships, love and commitment, as well as [for some] a sense of the Holy amongst us.[3]

This is something different from prescribed 'religion', and you certainly don't have to share the same faith as me to get something out of this book. For me, my faith is key to my wellbeing, but it isn't about black-and-white answers, or telling others what to think. I write my books not as an expert who has it all together, but as someone on a journey who is still learning and still processing. My hope is that my processing will help others on their journey too.

In our world today, I believe that, more than anything, we need some hope to hold on to. Matt Haig, in his brilliant *The Comfort Book*, tells the story of the famous song 'Over the Rainbow'. It is a bittersweet song, written by Harold Arlen and Yip Harburg in 1939. Yip, who wrote the lyrics, had not only seen the devastation of the First World War, but was also bankrupted in the Great Crash that happened in 1929. Harold, who wrote the melody, had lost a twin in infancy and fled his Jewish Orthodox parents at the age of sixteen to follow a musical path. It was here – against the background of Adolf Hitler targeting the Jewish population, in the midst of fear, uncertainty and anxiety – that one of the most hopeful songs ever written was born. The song has endured over decades and been covered countless times by many artists. A poignant one for me was Eva Cassidy, the singer who died so young of cancer, who bellowed it out with her acoustic guitar. In more recent years, Ariana Grande, at a memorial concert for the twenty-two victims of the 2017 Manchester bombings, choked back tears as she sang it. Many different cultures and generations joined with her in a beautiful picture of common humanity, holding on to hope after something so incredibly bleak.

Matt Haig wrote: 'Nothing is stronger than a small hope that doesn't give up.'[4]

The human spirit is incredible.

In this life or the next, I am believing for brighter days.

1
Honesty

Having bad mental health says nothing more about you than that you are human.

Showreels

I was standing next to the then Duke and Duchess of Cambridge (now Prince and Princess of Wales), facing a wall of photographers who were taking pictures of us as we smiled and chatted. Behind the photographers, a large crowd of onlookers cheered for this royal visit.

The Duke and Duchess were visiting XLP, a charity I had set up to help young people in inner-city London, and it looked like we'd made it. The photos would be all over social media in minutes, the footage on BBC News that evening, the story in the newspapers the following day and then in *Hello!* magazine in the coming weeks. As we shook hands and said our goodbyes, my phone started to light up.

> *Congratulations Patrick!*
> *This is amazing – you're doing so well!*
> *I can't believe you were hanging out with a future King and Queen!*
> *XLP has really made it!*

How it looked

My social media notifications were going crazy, with everyone excited to see the Royal Family showing their interest in, and support of, our work. This was the pinnacle of success, and if you looked at my smile, you'd probably think it was one of the happiest days of my life.

The news coverage showed the highlights reel: a successful day for a successful charity. But I could see behind the scenes. An hour or so after the furore had calmed down, I was sitting on my bed scrolling through my phone. There was no smile, just tears in my eyes.

How it felt

Although the charity looked like it was doing well, I was living in constant fear.

My anxiety was running wild, my heart constantly racing. I was exhausted and running on empty. I felt like I was falling, and I couldn't stop myself. There was nothing to hold on to, and there was no bottom to the hole I was falling into.

How did I end up here? It must be luck, a fluke – I don't deserve it.

One day everyone will know what I'm really like and everything will come crashing down.

Maybe people will stop giving if they think we're doing really well, and then we won't have enough money to pay the staff. Who will work with these young people and give them hope if we're not around any more?

Of course, it wasn't just about work. My life felt out of control as I awaited a hideously painful knee operation. The previous one had almost crushed me; now I had to go through it again.

I was ashamed. What would people think if they knew how bad my mental health was?

I was scared of being honest.

I felt alone.

Social media never tells the full story.

I had a choice: pretend to be living my best life, share all the news coverage and exaggerate the time I'd spent with the Duke and Duchess. Or be honest. Admit I didn't have it all together.

The first person I needed to admit it to?

Myself.

Instagram vs reality (things we don't shout about on social media)

The sunny landscape
The day it rained so hard you couldn't see out of the window

The pithy quote about self-confidence
The days of self-doubt, the tears and the meltdowns

The idealised beach body
The weeks of self-deprivation before posting; the weeks of self-doubt afterwards

The friendship group, holding drinks and grinning at the camera
The insecurities and doubts of *Do I belong here?*

The smiling family on holiday
The toddler meltdown two minutes later that ended the outing early

The podcast release
The months and years of hard work it took to get there

The happy couple having dinner at a nice restaurant
The fight they had beforehand about where to eat

Rethinking courage

What do you think about when someone says the word 'courage'?

I used to think of courage as heroic acts on the battlefield; the boxer who refuses to go down and reaches the final round; the single mum who keeps going when her partner has left her alone with small kids and a pile of debt.

I once posed this question on social media while sitting on the edge of my bed, exhausted and lonely. I couldn't have felt less courageous if I tried. I had no energy, no fight in me, and my heart sank as the expected responses appeared: 'Feel the fear and do it anyway!', 'Go against the flow!', 'Never say die!' Then, one phrase stood out from all the rest, offering me a scrap of hope: 'Courage is allowing yourself to be vulnerable.'

Vulnerability sounded weak and messy, but something about it grabbed my attention. I looked into it and came across the work of researcher and professor Brené Brown, who write: 'Vulnerability is not weakness; it's our greatest measure of courage.'[1]

Taking deep breaths, I read more of what she had to say on the subject in another of her books:

Owning our story can be hard but not nearly as difficult as spending our lives running from it. Embracing our vulnerabilities is risky but not nearly as dangerous as giving up on love and belonging and joy – the experiences that make us the most vulnerable. Only when we are brave enough to explore the darkness will we discover the infinite power of our light.[2]

I began to realise that real courage wasn't putting my head down and getting on with it; it wasn't stuffing my feelings into a box and pretending to the world that I was OK. No. It meant owning what was going on – *my story* – so I could get help. I had to swallow my pride because I was embarrassed to admit I was struggling.

I'd been saying I was fine, trying to keep my chin up, but that wasn't magically making things OK. I'd been pushing on when I was near the edge, hoping I could just keep going – even with nothing left in the tank.

The first thing I needed to do was tell my family and close friends the truth. I had been hiding what I was going through and had wound up isolated. In my pain, what I really needed was to know that, despite how I felt, I was still loved. I still had value. That there were people in my life who wouldn't judge me for feeling low but who could look at me, *the real me*, with no pretences or filters, and love me just as I was.

Honesty breeds honesty

I have known Peter for most of my life. Countless times we've seen each other and said, 'Hey, how are you?' The other would reply, 'Good. You?' 'Yep, OK thanks!'

Recently, we took part in a weekly wellbeing group together, in which we were encouraged to share some of the high and low points of our lives in pairs. Sitting next to each other, he began to talk, and I was taken aback. He'd faced so many challenges that I had never been aware of. 'I'm so sorry we've never spoken about this before,' I said. 'I had no idea.'

I reconsidered the more surface-level struggles I had planned on sharing. He'd been honest with me; perhaps I could do the same with him. I took a deep breath and began. As I spoke, he smiled and empathised. There was no judgement in his eyes or his words – just kindness and warmth. I realised honesty not only *takes* courage, but it *breeds* courage.

Positive vibes only

Everything happens for a reason!
Look on the bright side!
Everything always works out OK in the end!
Just have a positive mental attitude!

It sounds strange, but too much positivity can actually damage us. Of course, there's nothing wrong with being happy, but when we try to *pretend* we're happy and force ourselves to act cheerfully because we think our negative feelings are wrong, we're not helping anyone.

Many of us are already uncomfortable with the emotions we perceive as being negative. We don't want to be sad, fearful, uncomfortable, angry or envious... And then we see a slogan like 'Positive vibes only', and we think that's how we should be living. But those perceived negative emotions aren't wrong; they are just signals that are trying to communicate something to us. Psychotherapist Lori Gottlieb says: 'Our feelings are like a GPS system. They tell us what direction to go in, and if we pretend we're not feeling something, it's like walking around with a faulty GPS – you never know what direction to go in.'[3]

Feelings aren't our enemies that need to be squashed down, ignored, overridden and kept hidden. We can't run forever, and those emotions don't just disappear. Have you ever tried to hide your pain and then found you've become numb to what's going on around you? Have you been hurt but not felt able to express it and instead become sarcastic and snarky? Ever exploded in anger or burst into tears over something small, and known somewhere deep inside that you were reacting to far more than what just happened in the moment?

Not dealing with our emotions doesn't make *them* weaker; it makes *us* weaker. It doesn't make *us* stronger; it makes *the emotions* stronger.

Perhaps big boys and girls need to cry more often.

Pain Top Trumps

How can I complain about my pain when others have it far worse?

How many times do we tell ourselves that? We try to put our pain away, pretending it's not important. But hurt is hurt. Pain is pain.

The fact your sister has a migraine doesn't mean your headache stops. The fact there are people's lives that have been devastated by wars doesn't mean that being made redundant doesn't come with some real challenges. The fact others are grieving loved ones won't magic away your depression.

Edith Eger, psychologist, author and survivor of Auschwitz says:

> People say to me, 'Things in my life are pretty hard right now, but I have no right to complain – it's not *Auschwitz*.' This kind of comparison can lead us to minimize or diminish our own suffering. Being a survivor, being a 'thriver' requires absolute acceptance of what was and what is. If we discount our pain, or punish ourselves for feeling lost or isolated or scared about the challenges in our lives, however insignificant these challenges may seem to someone else, then we're still choosing to be victims. We're not seeing our choices. We're judging ourselves. I don't want you to hear my story and say, 'My own suffering is less significant.' I want you to hear my story and say, 'If she can do it, then so can I!'[4]

Telling ourselves, *It could be worse*, invalidates our feelings. Feeling grateful for the good things we have is helpful; telling ourselves the bad things aren't really that bad isn't.

Let's not play Top Trumps with our pain, but find some self-compassion.

What stops us from being honest?

Ever worried what someone might say if you were to tell them how you really feel? You're not alone. I asked some friends what makes it hard for them to be honest, and the most common answer was fear.

What are we scared of?

Being rejected
Being judged
People not liking us
Looking stupid
Being a burden
People not understanding
Feeling exposed
Looking like a failure
What if we're too much and people can't cope?
What if the person we confide in walks away?
What if others realise we're not who they thought we'd be?

There is so much fear surrounding this topic, because while we can choose whom we confide in, we can't choose how they respond.

Struggling with mental health says nothing more about you than that you're human. All humans have ups and downs; we all face different battles. It doesn't make us weak or unworthy of love. If someone rejects us or belittles how we feel, that says far more about them than it does about us. That doesn't magic away our fears, but understanding them can be the first step to overcoming them.

Which, if any, of the list above resonates with you? What truth can you hold on to when feeling this fear?

Lonely in a crowd

According to psychiatrist Carl Jung, 'Loneliness does not come from having no people about one, but from being unable to communicate the things that seem important to oneself, or from holding views which others find inadmissible.'[5]

The loneliest place to be is in a crowd of people when we don't feel like we can be our authentic selves. Fear tells us that, if we say what we're really feeling or thinking, our relationships with the people around us could change forever. So we stay quiet. We hide our fears and insecurities. We wrap up our dreams. We keep our thoughts reined in so that we stay palatable to those around us. And what happens?

We feel lonely. Unseen. Unheard. Disconnected.

We don't let down our barriers because we don't want to get hurt, which gives off the vibe that we don't want to connect with others. And so, we end up feeling even more lonely, unseen, unheard and disconnected. We're communicating that people should back off, when in reality we crave connection and belonging.

We need to find safe people we can talk to – whether it's a loved one, a therapist, or something like a Kintsugi Hope group. We all deserve someone who will listen to us, and show us empathy, compassion and kindness. Vulnerability isn't telling everyone everything. It is about choosing to let down our guard with a handful of trusted people.

When John joined one of our Kintsugi Wellbeing Groups, he'd had a series of failed relationships, Without a strong support network, his mental health deteriorated rapidly. He was self-harming, abusing drugs and alcohol, had disengaged with society, and was planning to take his own life. Joining a group meant he found a safe place where he could find the courage to be himself. He told me that our motto – 'Discovering treasure in life's scars' – was really helpful for him and made him see that it was OK not to be

OK. He started to see that his scars spoke of the battles he had been through and that he didn't need to be ashamed of them. Hearing other people's stories helped him see that he wasn't alone. Others were also going through hard things, and they could go through them together, supporting one another along the way.

Choose the ultimate act of courage. Find a safe person and be vulnerable. Tell them how you feel. I hope they prove themselves worthy of your time and love you wholeheartedly.

You deserve it.

Picking a safe person

Things that might be helpful to consider:

- ☐ Are they comfortable talking about their own feelings?
- ☐ Are they compassionate?
- ☐ Are they trustworthy?
- ☐ Do they respect boundaries?
- ☐ Do they keep people's confidences?
- ☐ Do they have the time to listen?
- ☐ Is it likely they will try to tell you what to do rather than hearing you out?
- ☐ Do you feel comfortable enough with them to let them know that you're not expecting them to resolve what's going on, but just to provide a listening ear?

I got a feeling

Spirituality is a huge part of wellbeing for millions of people across the globe, and though it sometimes comes with some unhelpful connotations, it shouldn't be ignored. The awareness of being connected to something bigger than ourselves can give us a sense of worth and purpose, and values to guide us on our life's path. When suffering enters our world, spirituality and faith can be a comfort, but can also cause us to ask questions: Why would God let this happen to me? How can he be good if he lets me go through this? It can eat away at our sense of connection with God, leaving us confused, weary and bruised. The answer isn't to turn away from spirituality; it's to find a place of honesty within it. There we will find true solace and comfort.

Many people of faith say that it was when they were at their lowest that they felt God closest, wrapping them in his love and helping them to get through their pain. That's a beautiful thing. But for me, when I was going through what felt like hell, I couldn't have felt like God was further away.

I was in physical pain from a huge operation where surgeons broke my leg and pinned it back together. I wore a huge circular frame that was helping to reset the bones. It was agony to wear, and of course made moving pretty difficult. Each night Diane would adjust the struts that penetrated my bones, and it was torturous.

I would shout at God: 'Please! I can't do this any more. It's too hard! The lack of sleep, the inability to walk, the effort to keep my emotions in check when I just want to shout and scream.' There was no response; nothing changed. I just plodded on, trying to hold on to my sanity and my faith when both felt like they were ebbing away. Perhaps God didn't like me.

Someone who helped me grapple with this was Sir Terry Waite. Terry was held hostage for five years in Beirut after being taken prisoner in 1987 while working to release other hostages. He had been working as part of the Archbishop of Canterbury's envoy. He spent 1,460 days in solitary confinement, and wasn't released for almost another year. The conditions he describes were horrific. Held in a cell, chained to a wall and sleeping on the floor, he had no natural light, no companionship and nothing to read, watch or listen to in order to dull the agonising passage of time. It is impossible to imagine the anguish of such conditions, especially when he didn't know if, or when, he might be released, or whether he would be held there until his execution.

Terry says that one day he was told he had five hours left to live. His captors allowed him to write one letter to his loved ones and to say the Lord's Prayer, then they held a gun to his head. Believing he was seconds from death, having risked his life to help other people, he says: 'I felt alone and isolated. I never felt what some people claim to feel: the close presence of God. That doesn't mean to say I lost faith, because faith is not dependent on feeling. Feeling can be occasioned by illness and all sorts of things, but it's not a reliable guide as to whether you have faith.

'But I could say, in the face of my captors, "You have the power to break my body by beating me, you have the power to bend my mind by interrogating me, but my soul is not yours to possess."'[6]

This is not to say that feelings are unimportant, but I have come to agree with Terry that they are not always a reliable guide as to whether we have faith. I have started to see that real faith isn't one that says it never encounters doubts or discouragements, but instead, is real in the face of them. My spirituality is crucial to my wellbeing, and I can be honest with God. I don't have to hide how I'm feeling or what I'm thinking.

Faith isn't black and white; it's full of questions and mystery. I'm learning to be OK with that, and to remember that no matter how it feels, I'm never on my own.

Embracing the journey

If you could draw a line representing your life so far, with all of its ups and downs, what would it look like?

Here's mine...

You can draw yours here...

Look at some of the low points you've already been through and think about what helped you when you were in that place. What were some of the things that moved you on to a better place? How could those things help you now?

It pays to pinpoint

The more accurately we can pinpoint our emotions, the more easily we can discern what is causing them and begin to deal with them. Try this exercise:

In recent weeks and months, I have regularly felt... (*Circle or make a note of the emotions below that you remember experiencing*):

Angry	Grateful
Anxious	Guilty
Ashamed	Happy
Bored	Hopeful
Calm	Hurt
Confused	Jealous
Content	Joyful
Depressed	Overwhelmed
Desperate	Proud
Disappointed	Resentful
Discouraged	Resigned
Disgusted	Sad
Envious	Stressed
Excited	Surprised
Expectant	Vulnerable
Fearful	

What stands out to you as a you look at this list?

Writing the wrongs

Write down here, in a journal or on a piece of paper, how you are really feeling. Be honest with yourself; don't hold back. This is just for you, so no one else ever has to see it. You don't have to write poetic sentences. Bullet points, single words and random thoughts can be just as cathartic!

It's good to talk

Find someone you feel safe with and have a chat. Take a step of vulnerability and see how you feel afterwards. Perhaps make a note of it here.

Deeper conversations

Ask some intentional questions that help your conversations go beyond the surface, such as:

1 What's making you happy at the moment?
2 How are you looking after your mental health?
3 What are you thankful for?
4 What's worrying you right now?
5 What have been your strongest emotions this week? What are they trying to tell you?
6 If you're the praying sort, what prayer would you love to see answered?

Remember Tetris?

For the young and uninitiated, *Tetris* is a computer game, popular in the 1980s, where blocks of different shapes and sizes fall from the 'sky', and you need to rotate the shapes using the keyboard to get them into a straight line before they hit the bottom of the screen. When a line is complete it disappears, and you then start working on your next line. The longer the game goes on, the faster the blocks start falling, until you begin bashing your keyboard as fast as you can, but not quite getting them in a straight line quickly enough… which means that before long they are all piling up, reaching the top, and it is GAME OVER.

My journey with anxiety has often felt like a game of *Tetris*. Anxiety-inducing events always seem to come at once. I can feel like I'm just dealing with one thing, when straight away another thing goes wrong, another block starts to fall, and then another and another.

When I first voiced how I was feeling, people said, 'Try mindfulness,' or, 'CBT is good,' or, 'Do more exercise, that will help,' or – my personal favourite and one often heard within some of the Christian communities I've been a part of over the years – 'Try praying harder.' I knew those people had good intentions, but they didn't realise that the blocks were falling so quickly that it was tough to even think straight, let alone use logic. I felt out of control, my mind racing, my heart thumping, my stomach in knots. It was like falling into a black hole, desperately trying to grab hold of something but grasping at air, feeling scared and alone. I felt guilty that I couldn't seem to employ the techniques everyone told me would help, which led to a spiral of feeling like a terrible person – a failure – because I couldn't just 'snap out of it'. I thought my family deserved better. What kind of a husband and father was I?

Let me be clear: cognitive behavioural therapy (CBT), mindfulness, therapy, exercise, prayer and healthy lifestyle changes are all good things, and I will share some of the techniques I have found helpful in this chapter, but a real game-changer for me was realising that **anxiety is not weakness**. In fact, I now know that people who struggle with anxiety, but who still carry on, are some of the most courageous people I've met. They show up despite their struggles; they are kind, sensitive and have huge amounts of empathy for others – even when they feel like there is a car alarm constantly going off in their minds.

Writer Kirsten Corley shares that 'anxiety is the most caring person in the room',[1] and her words struck a chord with me. She pointed out how many times we worry because we care – because we don't want to hurt someone or let them down. We don't want our own hearts to be hurt. We don't want to make the wrong choice and therefore find ourselves paralysed. Anxiety tells us we'll ruin everything we touch, we'll fail at everything we try, we'll hurt other people. Kirsten reminded me that we're all human and that: 'Anxiety is that want and need to be everyone's hero but you have to remember to save yourself sometimes.'[2] In short, she helped me to see that anxiety is normal, and it doesn't make me a bad person.

If you struggle with anxiety, I want you to know that you are loved, you are valued, and you have a massive contribution to make to the world. You aren't weak. Chances are, your anxiety comes from a place of caring deeply.

I know that when I went to the doctor for some medication, I felt like a failure, despite being aware that taking a tablet for anxiety was no different from taking a tablet for a headache. In part, it was the little voice that kept saying to me:

My life isn't that hard.
I should be able to beat this.
I must be stronger.
I ought to have learned all the techniques by now.
Not a nice voice, is it?

Anxiety feels like...

- I'm the tiny little ball in a pinball game being tossed from one anxious thought to the next one without a minute to process.
- A train is running in my mind, hurtling down the tracks, and I can't stop it or get off.
- My body is on fire.
- A constant churning of thoughts I can't control, my heart pounding and an overwhelming feeling of frustration.
- My mind running at light speed while everything around me is in slow motion.
- A sense there's something bad coming, but I don't know what it is.
- Being numb, stuck and unable to make decisions.
- My whole body shuts down while my mind races.
- Mental toothache. A throbbing, peace-stealing, constant pain that occasionally eases (inexplicably), only to come back with a vengeance.
- My body isn't my own. I feel dizzy, sick and can't eat.
- All I want to do is to cancel my plans and stay safe inside.
- I can't find rest – emotionally, physically, spiritually or mentally.
- Overthinking and dwelling on worst-case scenarios.
- Constantly bracing myself for the next 'hit'.
- There are 100 tabs open in the computer of my mind, all screaming for attention so my mind can't focus on any one of them. I want to switch the whole thing off and sleep, but my mind won't let me.
- Living at breaking point – like an elastic band stretched to maximum.[3]

Managing anxiety

Our instinct when it comes to anxiety can be to fight it, to try to reject every negative thought that comes into our heads, and to avoid situations or people that make us feel anxious. But is that really possible, and is it really helping us? As Carl Jung pointed out in his writings, the harder we try not to think about something, the more we find ourselves thinking about it. We have to find another route through our anxieties.

As I was working through my own struggles with anxiety, it really helped me to understand the difference between resignation and acceptance. Resignation is a feeling of being defeated; of knowing that things aren't as we want them to be, but feeling as if they are inevitable and that they will never change. Acceptance, on the other hand, means that instead of beating yourself up about your feelings, you accept that it is how you feel and know that it's OK. It means acknowledging that your feelings are data, telling you something is going on that needs to be addressed. This is a more compassionate response that means you stay out of self-judgement and respond by being curious about what is causing your feelings, and what they are trying to tell you about your life and circumstances. You remove the guilt of not being able to simply push those thoughts and feelings away.

Acceptance allows you to hold on to hope. You're not resigning yourself to a life of worry; you're just being realistic about how you're feeling now, while balancing that with the fact that you will likely feel better at some point in the future. Anxiety doesn't need to be a life sentence. It may not disappear completely, but there is always hope that we can change.

Chloe Brotheridge, author of *The Anxiety Solution*, talks about the idea of floating with anxiety rather than fighting against it. She uses the metaphor of being at sea. Not being a great swimmer, you struggle and thrash around, which leaves you exhausted and barely able to keep your head above water. In contrast, she says we should try to imagine what would happen if you we were to lie back and relax. Your body would be able to float without any effort on your part. She writes:

> What would it be like to just allow the thoughts and sensations of anxiety to be there, without trying to control them or make them stop? To 'float' with anxiety rather than to fight it? By letting go and allowing the feelings to be there without needing to push them away, you stop the fight and the symptoms pass all by themselves. If what you resist persists, then what you allow dissolves.[4]

Another way to think about it is like an annoying guest at a party. Once they're there, you have a choice: you can seethe about their presence and focus on every irritating thing they do, or you can accept they're there and get on with your night. You're not able to completely ignore them, but neither is your whole night shaped or ruined by them. You might even find they have some redeeming qualities after all.[5]

Unhelpful things to say to someone who struggles with anxiety...

- You'll be fine!
- Don't worry. Everyone gets nervous from time to time.
- Cheer up – things could be worse.
- Get over it.
- It's all in your head.
- At least… (followed by absolutely anything).
- Why don't you just look on the bright side?
- Here's a colouring book!
- What do you have to feel anxious about?
- You can *choose* not to be anxious.
- God won't give you more than you can handle.
- I'm lucky I don't struggle with anxiety; I'm quite strong like that.
- Worrying gets you nowhere.
- It's been a while. Shouldn't you be over it by now?
- You have a victim mentality.
- You just need to focus on the good things in your life.

Helpful things to say to someone who has anxiety...

- I'm here any time you need me.
- Your feelings are valid.
- Take one step at a time, one breath at a time.
- Don't belittle yourself because of the way you are feeling.
- That sounds hard.
- I'll stay with you.
- I don't understand how you feel, but I'm here to listen if you want to talk.
- You're seen. You're heard.
- What would be helpful for you in this moment?
- There is no rush... You don't have to perform according to someone else's schedule.
- It's OK to not be OK.

Squashing it down

It is impossible to avoid trauma. Even if we are not the ones going through it, we can often witness it and inhale the second-hand smoke of traumatic events taking place all around us. Most of us will experience three or four traumatic events in our lifetime, but a friend of mine, John Sutherland, a former borough commander in Southwark and Camden, told me that during their careers, each police officer is likely to encounter between 400 and 600.

The first trauma in John's policing career occurred when he attended a domestic murder scene. That was early on in his role. After that, he had to negotiate during an armed siege, tell distraught parents that their child had been killed, and attend the scene of many fatal road traffic accidents. For years he tucked it all deep inside, burying the emotion and heartbreak so he could continue in his role.

Then, after twenty years, everything changed.

All the emotional turmoil caught up with him, and he went from being an active London borough commander to being overwhelmed with exhaustion. Not an 'I-need-a-holiday' type of tired, but a bone-deep, life-crippling exhaustion. He would wake in the middle of the night gripped by panic for no discernible reason. Then he was engulfed in depression, which he describes as 'a waterboarding of the mind'. For seven months he was unable to work. Some days he was unable to do little more than lie on the sofa and breathe. A combination of medication, counselling and rest helped him get back on his feet and begin to focus on getting better. We need to stop pretending that we don't have needs and that things don't affect us. We need to be aware of our privileges, while recognising the trauma we have experienced and been exposed to, and the impact it's had on us. We need safe spaces to process – with friends, family and often therapists. We can't live lives untouched by traumatic events, but we can build safety nets to help us deal with them.

Anxiety says...

That person at work didn't talk to me much today; they must be disappointed with me.

Reality: They had an argument with their boyfriend and were distracted.

They didn't text me back; I knew they didn't really like me.

Reality: Their phone battery died.

The kids aren't home yet; I'm sure something awful has happened.

Reality: The train was running late.

I upset them and now they hate me.

Reality: What you said did upset them, but they don't hate you. Things can be worked out, and conflict is part of human relationships.

Control

Worrying about problems we can't fix can leave us feeling frustrated, anxious and powerless. We may feel as if we have very little control in life, but there is always something we can control – even if it is just our reaction to our circumstances.

Try this. Get a pen and a piece of paper, and draw two circles, one inside the other.

In the outer circle, put all the things you are worrying about but can't control. Things like: who you're related to, the weather, the mood your boss will be in tomorrow, when someone might die, natural disasters, politicians, the past, the future. You get the picture!

In the inner circle, put the things you can control that relate to those worries. For example, if you're worried about how someone might treat you, you can't control that, but you can control your response and your own boundaries. If you're worried about your health, you can't guarantee you don't have anything to worry about, but you can choose to go and see a doctor.

There's a lot in this world that we can't control, but we can control our actions and reactions, how kind we are to ourselves, whether we choose to forgive people or hold on to grudges, whether we choose to let others in, and more. This isn't an exercise in pretending the worries aren't real; the idea is to help us focus less on what we can't control and more on what we can, so we feel less impotent.

Take the thought to court

What is the key thought that is causing you anxiety at the moment? Write it down, then 'put in in the dock'.

Write down the evidence that this thought is true, aiming for hard facts.

Now, cross-examine the thought. Is it opinion or fact? What evidence suggests it's true?

Looking at both sides, come up with a 'closing statement' that provides a balanced overview based on all the evidence.

What could be an alternative thought?

Struggling to sleep?

I used to lie in bed for hours feeling anxious, tossing and turning, trying everything I could think of to get some precious sleep. Then someone told me this brilliant tip: if you can't sleep after twenty minutes, get up and do something else. Try not to do anything stimulating, but perhaps make a non-caffeinated drink, read a favourite book, listen to some calming music and head back to bed when you feel yourself getting sleepy. When in bed, close your eyes and picture a walk you've done many times. Mentally take yourself on that walk, noticing all the detail you can from the moment you put on your shoes and leave the house, right through to the sounds and smells as you walk. Keep doing the same mental walk each night, and your mind will begin to associate it with relaxation and going to sleep.

Stress bucket

A build-up of stress is bad news for anxiety, so understanding what increases and decreases our stress is a really helpful tool.

Though there may be some common things that stress us out, we're all wired differently and all respond to things in different ways. Diane, my wife and co-founder of the charity we lead, Kintsugi Hope, loves the challenge of dealing with difficult emails and phone calls because she thrives on finding creative solutions. I hate that, but come alive when I am involved in public speaking, which she finds incredibly stressful.

The stress bucket is an idea used in the brilliant Mental Health First Aid England[6] training, which helps us to understand what causes us stress, what relieves our stress and how we can keep things in a healthy balance. Several times I've come back to this tool and written down what is currently causing me stress. Things that affect me tend to include:

- Illnesses
- My children facing challenges
- Lack of exercise owing to my knee condition
- Financial issues
- Consistent work pressure

All those things can lead to my bucket being very full, which makes my anxiety worse and harder to manage.

Warning signs for me are that I start to take things too personally and snap at people with little provocation. Then I know something is wrong, and I need to address the balance. For others, warning signs might be feeling tearful, exhausted or burnt out.

What do we need to do when this happens?

Release some of the stress using the tap at the bottom of the bucket. This tap represents our coping mechanisms, things that help keep us calm, which will, like the stresses, vary from person to person. For me, things that help include:

- Walking
- Reading
- Listening to music
- Catching up with a close friend
- Watching football (though depending on the score, this can have the opposite effect!)

Understanding ourselves better and building effective strategies to deal with stress can only help in our battles to manage anxiety.

Grounding

Here are five simple exercises for when you feel panic rising.

5, 4, 3, 2, 1

Breathe deeply, in through your nose and out of your mouth. Then slowly look around and find:

   5 things you can see,
   4 things you can touch,
   3 things you can hear,
   2 things you can smell,
   1 thing you can taste.

Touch

Pick up or touch some items that are near you. Focus on how they feel: Cool or warm? Soft or scratchy? Heavy or light? Think about their colour: try to be specific, using words such as *crimson* or *burgundy* rather than *red*.

Move

Walk, stretch, jump or jog, and as you do, think about how your body feels with each movement.

Categories

Think of a category, such as musical instruments, ice cream flavours or football teams. Mentally list as many things as you can within that category over a minute or two. Alternatively, pick a number of categories and name your favourite three things within each one.

Visualise

Think about your favourite place: a room in your home, a place you've been on holiday, a friend's garden. Imagine you're there. What do you see, hear, smell? Think about the last time you were there. What did you do, and how did it feel?[7]

Serenity Prayer

Grant me the serenity to accept the things I cannot change,
Courage to change the things I can,
And wisdom to know the difference[8]

Strong for too long

There are many factors that may contribute towards someone getting depression. For me, it came on slowly and was affected by a large number of stressful events that built up over many years.

When I was in my twenties, I began working with young people who were at risk of being excluded. Knife crime and poverty were their norm, and I felt led to start my own charity to be able to support them more meaningfully. I loved working with the young people, but found it a slog to be continually raising money to keep the charity going and trying to find solutions to the insurmountable problems our community was facing. I didn't know how to set good boundaries; I felt like everything was on my shoulders, and I just needed to work, work, work. In addition, there was always a little voice in my head saying I was nothing special, and at some point I'd be found out for playing at being a charity CEO.

Over the years, I got angry. Angry at the injustices in my community, angry at the systemic issues that kept the kids in these difficult situations, angry at those who didn't seem to notice what was going on or care about what was happening, often on their own doorstep. I didn't know how to express that anger in healthy ways, so I bottled it up and turned it inwards.

Diane and I married young and started a family, and I desperately wanted to be a good husband and dad. The pressure of work didn't stop, so I just added family life into the mix. I didn't feel like I deserved to rest when there was always so much to do. Our eldest daughter developed a rare condition (Henoch-Schönlein purpura, or HSP), which caused her a huge amount of pain and meant we were regularly rushing in and out of hospital, hoping the doctors would be able to find some combination of medication to keep her symptoms under control. Around the same time, my dad went into hospital with bowel cancer for what was, on paper, a routine operation. After multiple complications he ended up staying in for nine weeks, having four operations and losing three stone in weight.

Before too long I was getting ready for my own operations for a degenerative knee condition and had to face major limb reconstruction surgery twice. I felt like all my prayers were going unanswered (things seemed to get worse rather than better), and I was frustrated with myself, believing it was all my fault and I should be able to fix myself. On my dark days I felt like people would be better off if I wasn't around. These types of thoughts helped me realise I was depressed; in fact, I was at rock bottom and needed help.

There are lots of reasons people don't seek help when they are depressed, including shame, stigma and inertia. For me, it was that I didn't believe I was worthy of help. When a kind friend offered to pay for me to see a psychologist, I couldn't think of anything worse. Sit opposite a stranger who wanted to poke around in my past? No, thank you. (My idea of psychologists came more from films than any sort of reality.) Reluctantly, however, I figured that things were already so bad, what did I have to lose?

At that first meeting, as I described my situation, the psychologist said, 'I'm not at all surprised you're struggling, given the combinations of events that have happened to you.' That blew my mind! There had to be a reason I was feeling the way I was, and I was convinced it was my fault. She continued: 'Struggling doesn't make you a failure; it makes you a human being. You need to be kind to yourself, as you've been through a lot.' I am not entirely sure what I was expecting, but it wasn't that.

At first, I thought there might be a magic answer. 'How many sessions until I feel better?' I asked. She kindly explained that it takes a long time to turn a massive ocean liner around. There is no quick fix. She said I needed to learn to manage my thinking and to balance my thoughts, and that this would take time and practice, especially as I have a sensitive nature.

Wendy Bray and Chris Ledger, authors of *Insight into Depression*, write:

> Having a sensitive character, or a spirit, which readily responds to the needs of others, is a wonderful gift. But the flipside of that gift is that we are vulnerable to the thoughtlessness, rudeness, spite and bad temper of others. It isn't enough to 'toughen up' or 'develop a thicker skin'. Criticism can hurt – and hurt deeply. We may feel trampled on, wounded and rejected. If that hurt remains, unhealed… it can lead to depression.[1]

Maybe I wasn't weak for not being able to shrug things off. Maybe it didn't make me a bad person that I was struggling! I started reading more, keen to learn about this disease that I was starting to realise I had completely misunderstood. Dr Tim Cantopher, author of *Depressive Illness*,[2] said he has found that patients with clinical depression nearly always show:

- Moral strength
- Reliability
- Diligence
- A strong conscience
- A strong sense of responsibility
- A tendency to focus on the needs of others before their own

This was a far cry from my perception of depression as being about weakness and failings, a lack of courage and a sign of selfishness. Alongside the sessions with my psychologist, books like this began to help me understand myself. I slowly started to realise that this journey of healing and self-discovery was one I would be on for life.

Myths about depression

It's all in your head.

If you're clinically depressed, you can't just 'get over it' or distract yourself the way you sometimes can when you feel sad. It is a medical condition that requires medical attention.

It's always brought on by a traumatic event.

Losing someone you love, being lonely, losing a job or a dream, or circumstances such as not being able to have children can increase your risk of becoming depressed, but they aren't always the sole trigger.

Depression is a normal part of life.

While sadness is a universal experience, depression isn't something anyone should have to 'put up with'. Help is available, and with the right support, it is possible to manage the illness.

If you have a family member with depression, you'll get it too.

There is a slightly increased risk of getting depression if a family member has had it, but it's only a small factor. It's wise to be aware of your family's medical history, but don't assume that because someone else has had it you automatically will.

If you take antidepressants, you will have to be on them for life.

Doctors will recommend the appropriate dosage and length of prescription for each individual. They will sometimes prescribe therapy alongside medication to help ease and manage symptoms.

Only women get depressed.

Men might be less likely to talk about their feelings and mental state, but that doesn't mean they don't get depressed. In England, three times as many men die by suicide than women, so trying to hide our feelings isn't strong – it can be life-threatening.[3]

Symptoms and signs of depression that are rarely talked about:

- Anger, aggression and starting fights
- Dissociation, obsessive thinking and paranoia
- Brain fog/cognitive impairment/memory loss
- Fatigue/exhaustion, even after eight hours' sleep
- Feeling overwhelmed and like you want to give up
- Feeling isolated, distant and detached from the world
- Staying away from people, fearing they won't understand you
- Loss of appetite
- Shutting down/withdrawing
- Small things like brushing your teeth, washing your hair or having a shower feeling like mountains to climb
- Irritation with everyone and everything
- Guilt and shame
- Mood swings
- Overcompensating – feeling like you have to become the life of the party when surrounded by others to hide how low you're feeling
- Sweating, palpitations
- Lack of motivation
- Wanting someone else to make your decisions, as it's less effort
- Being comfortable in your depression because it is familiar
- Low/nonexistent libido, which has an impact on a relationship
- Wanting help, but not wanting to burden people
- Randomly sobbing; not just crying, but body-shaking sobbing for no reason
- Feeling overstimulated by noise
- Sitting around, unable to move – just sitting staring into space
- Losing touch with friends
- Being around people but still feeling alone
- Numbness – like being sucked into a black hole you can't escape
- Lack of patience
- Dark and intrusive thoughts

Small steps are still steps

Days after my first knee operation, everything felt so dark. Depression can make you feel as if everything is hopeless and there will be no relief. This is often the same for those who love us but feel powerless to help.

I could see that Diane was really struggling, and I felt powerless to do anything as she ran upstairs looking like she was about to burst into tears. She told me later she'd gone into our bedroom and cried out: 'This is just too hard!' She could see no light at the end of this tunnel. I wasn't going to be fixed in a few days or even weeks, and she felt like the end was too far away to be of any comfort.

Sometimes it seems like a brighter day will never appear.

As she let out her pain and frustration, she suddenly felt a sense that she needed to stop looking for the light at the end of the tunnel and instead look for the light all around her. It wasn't the light of an end to all our troubles; it was the light of family, friends and neighbours who were surrounding us with so much love and kindness. The light was coming through pinprick holes in the darkness of the time, but it was light nonetheless.

She came downstairs with a renewed sense of purpose and determination, telling me what she'd discovered. I agreed that to survive we had to focus on getting through the hour in front of us, then the next hour, holding on to the light around us, not just waiting for the dark time to end. The key to recovery is to see that there is a flicker of light, no matter how dark it can feel.

'Just one candle' by Jane Smith

A glimmer of hope
Is what we need
In our time of pain.
Just one candle
Bringing light
To cheer us
Once again.
Day after day
Things stay the same
With no end in sight.
These winter nights
Dark and cold,
Longing for
Warm sunlight.
Our hearts break
With anguish
Beyond description.

How much longer
Must we wait
For hope of
Transformation.
Overwhelmed by
Grief and sadness,
Loss and sorrow,
Desperate for
The dawn to break
On a new
Tomorrow.
But if we light
Just one candle
Darkness is dispelled.
Gazing on
That flickering flame
May our hearts
Be stilled.[4]

Sadness vs depression

'We use "depressed" as a synonym for "sad", which is fine, as we use "starving" as a synonym for "hungry", though the difference between depression and sadness is the difference between genuine starvation and feeling a bit peckish.'[5]

Sadness

Normal reaction to loss and disappointment.

Part of healthy emotions.

Shows you care.

Can be temporary.

Often triggered by an event.

Depression

Mental illness, abnormal emotional state.

Can last a long time.

Leaves you feeling worthless and hopeless.

Makes you lose interest in things and people.

Can be isolating.

Can cause feelings of unreasonable guilt.

Can cause fatigue, irritability, and difficulty in sleeping and concentrating.

Can lead to suicidal thoughts.

Hope against hope

An hour-long documentary about *deserts*?! How on earth (no pun intended) could they have found an hour's worth of material? To me, a desert was a lifeless wasteland where you would only want to spend a minimal amount of time. Then I heard David Attenborough's distinctive narration talking about how deserts can be teeming with life...

When struggling with depression, the world can feel like a hopeless place, a desert where nothing seems to change. You have very little energy to do anything, and you feel beaten – not by the sun or the heat, but by life's circumstances and the negative thoughts going through your brain. Though it can feel desperate, it's not a life sentence. With the right support we can come through it and learn to manage our symptoms.

Watching that documentary reminded me of a phrase I'd heard since I was young: 'hope against hope'. It means to hope, very strongly, that something will happen, although you know it is not likely. The expression was used in the Bible when describing Abraham's desire that his wife Sarah would get pregnant, even though she was long past child-bearing age.[6] It reminds me that hope is a decision I make even when there doesn't seem to be supporting evidence. It's something I can choose to cling to whatever the circumstances.

If you're feeling hopeless – about how you feel yourself or on behalf of someone you love – let me be the one to say that there is always hope. *Always.*

Author David B. Seaburn writes:

Embattled hope... keeps its balance and continues to believe that there are possibilities awaiting us, opportunities, prospects, and potentialities, though hidden, that may materialize, come to life, and take hold if only by inches at first, then feet, then yards, then miles. It accepts that the odds may not be good, but insists on pushing through.[7]

Hope isn't denial. It's facing the bleakness and getting up day after day, knowing that one day things will change and there is always a reason to keep going.

SEEK LIFT

I found this exercise really helpful as a way to start facing my depression and finding a means to move through it.

SEEK
See the bigger picture
Exercise regularly
Enjoy – plan fun and creativity
Kindness to yourself
LIFT
Look after your body
Interact – connect with others
Find meaning
Take notice

See the bigger picture

Depression can feel all-consuming, but it is not who we are or the full picture of our lives. If you were to watch five minutes of a film and make all your judgements about the characters in that five minutes, it is likely that you would jump to some wrong conclusions. Where you are now is just one chapter of your life, so what's the rest of your story? Can you step back from how you feel and think? What would a friend say about your situation?

Exercise regularly

Playing football was a brilliant form of stress relief for me until my knee operations meant I could no longer run. Getting a dog encouraged me to get out of the house, even on my lowest days. Some days it took everything I had to get out of the door, but I realised it was an important sign to my family that I wanted to get better. Keeping ourselves mobile and taking regular exercise can help to increase energy levels, diminish stress and boost mood.

We don't need to spend hours doing something we hate. Find an activity you enjoy and do it, even if it's only for five minutes a day.

Enjoy – plan fun and creativity

Planning ahead can be tough when you think you won't be well enough to enjoy going on holiday, to the cinema or out for a meal. One of the things that stopped me wanting to plan good things was my fear that my presence would stop other people enjoying themselves. Taking my boys to watch Premier League football was something I loved, and making sure I went ahead and booked it in, regardless of how I felt or how worried I was, always gave me a lift.

Kindness to yourself

We talk to ourselves more than we talk to any other person. Ever. It's not possible to overestimate the power of speaking kindly and positively to yourself, just as you would to a friend. Instead of heaping guilt on yourself and picking over your perceived faults, what would a more compassionate approach look like? What if you were to focus on some of your strengths? Try treating yourself the same way you would a friend you love, and see how much it helps.

Look after your body

The leader on a mental health first aid course asked group members to raise their hand if they were self-harming. My immediate thought was, 'Wow, I wonder who would be brave enough to put their hand up!' No one did. Then she said, 'Who sometimes drinks too much to take the edge off the day?' Most hands went up. 'Who, when under pressure, spends more than they can afford on things they don't need, then feels stress in their bodies?' 'Who eats too much or too little to ease the pain?' The list went on until finally she asked again, 'Who self-harms?' Every hand in the room went up.

We all have coping mechanisms, but it's good to ask: what does my body need right now? How can I really take care of myself?

Eating healthily and regularly, getting enough sleep and taking prescribed medications are all good ways to look after our bodies.

Interact – connect with others

As an introvert, I get energy from being on my own, and when I'm struggling I particularly want to hide away, but even introverts need to spend time with others. Some days it may be just being in contact on social media or by WhatsApp; other times it's coffee with a friend. Regardless, connection always helps.

Find meaning

I have always wanted to believe that none of our experiences is wasted; that what we learn along the way often helps others. That's why I love writing. I always hope that something I write will help people feel less alone. I have received so many emails saying how important the books have been in people's healing and recovery, or how the books have helped them understand others going through a tough time. People have even said the books came to them during such a rough period it actually saved their life.

I am not sure I would have chosen some of the more difficult experiences in my life, but I am so grateful that nothing is wasted. Out of some of the worst times Kintsugi Hope was born, which now enables thousands of people to find safe places where they can be real and honest with one another. All of us can help other people; all of us have things we're passionate about. We don't need to break world records or go down in the history books. Living out what's important to us and thinking about how we want to be remembered can make a big difference.

Take notice

I can notice my thoughts and get curious about why I am thinking a certain way instead of judging them instantly. Perhaps I am overtired, hungry or feeling let down. Writing my thoughts out or discussing them with a close friend often helps, but pretending they are not there means they persist until I take notice.[8,9]

Where is your faith?

Struggling with depression made me feel like a fraud. Maybe you can relate. How many of us have said, 'I'm fine,' when really we're anything but? And how about those of us who have put on a brave face to attend a social event when the kindest thing we could have done for ourselves would have been to stay at home? Thank goodness that, as someone who identifies as a Christian, I had a supportive church community and faith in a higher power to help me. Well... not *exactly*.

During times of deep depression, I have too often found my faith adding to the fraudulent feelings rather than taking them away. *Surely as someone who claims to have a faith, I should be able to pray this away?* Church became a lonely place, where I felt like I was on the outside with all my mess – looking in at a group of people who appeared to have their lives together. The guilt was crushing: how could I claim to be a Christian and yet have so little faith? Surely God was fed up with me. Perhaps he was even punishing me.

I slowly discovered that faith isn't about the absence of doubt; it is about having somewhere to go with your questions, your anger, your tears. In fact, when I read the book of Psalms, I realised that the Bible doesn't shy away from the truth that life is a mixture of beauty and fragility. Forty per cent of these psalms are laments – heart-wrenching cries for God to do something to get the writers out of the moment they had found themselves in. In their laments, these writers chose to engage with God in their pain instead of either ignoring him, pinning on a smile or dressing up in their 'Sunday best'.

I felt encouraged that the Bible didn't shy away from the topic of depression either, showing that central characters like Elijah, Job, Jeremiah and King David all suffered from it. King David was the one who wrote Psalm 23, which is often read at weddings and funerals. Verse 4 says: 'Even though I walk through the darkest valley, I will fear no evil, for you are with me', and that reminds me that God doesn't signpost me around the darkest valleys in my life; he chooses to go there with me. That's what faith means to me now: that even when I feel alone, I know that my God is always with me.

Supporting Eeyore

One of the things that many people have come to love about Eeyore's part in the *Winnie the Pooh* stories is that, although he is always sad, his friends seem to accept him just as he is. They include him in their adventures. They don't try to change him or ask him to cheer up, and they don't modify their behaviour around him. Tigger still happily bounces around and Pooh is still a 'silly old bear', but they let Eeyore be who he is, on his terms.

When someone is depressed, it can be easy to bounce in and think we're helping by trying to cheer them up or to leave them be because it feels hard to be around them, but it's a game-changer if we just let them be themselves – no pressure. To allow them to talk if they want to talk, but not to force them to if they don't.

We can love people without trying to change or fix them. I'm learning that I am not the rescuer. It's not down to me to save everyone. I'm also not supposed to be the sponge for everyone else's pain. It's too much to carry. What I can be is a gentle presence in my friends' lives; someone who can create space for them, love them and not judge them.

4

Shame

Never allow your shame to tell you that you are not worthy of connection, belonging and love.

Guilt vs shame

Guilt and shame are two very different things.

Guilt says, 'I did something wrong.' Shame says, 'I am wrong.'

Although guilt makes us feel bad, we can feel guilty about our actions or behaviours but still believe we are a good person. Shame, however, makes us believe that we are worthless and undeserving. It attacks the very core of who we are.

Guilt can be healthy – it can drive us to change the way we act and make amends for things we've done. Shame is the opposite – it is extremely toxic. It serves no beneficial purpose, and we'd be much healthier if we moved towards compassion, which says that our mistakes don't define us; and acceptance, which reminds us that we can learn from our mistakes.

Whac-A-Mole

I used to love trips to the seaside as a kid where, after a day on the beach, we'd wind up playing games on the pier. Whac-A-Mole was my favourite. It's the one where you grab a rubber hammer, and every time a mole pops up on the board you have to bash it down. The mole would appear in different holes, so you'd have to keep your wits about you to anticipate its next strike, and, of course, it got faster and faster until it became almost impossible to whack. I always found it so satisfying at the start, being able to bash the mole and see it disappear, but then I inevitably ended up sweaty and stressed when I couldn't keep up with it!

In the book *The Power of Belonging*, my good friends Will van der Hart and Dr Rob Waller use the Whac-A-Mole game as an illustration of how life can feel when we're trying to fit in:

> The search for belonging can just be like 'Whac-A-Mole' in which we try to defeat each obstacle to belonging as it shows its head. We hit appearance, career, social life, church activity, academic credentials... We smash the inner blockages of worry, perfectionism, anger, guilt... But no matter how many 'moles' we whack, our sense of unbelonging persists... We need a deep solution that goes beyond the symptoms. The central mechanism is shame, a complex and often unaddressed emotion.[1]

We need to stop the moles from constantly appearing by turning the machine off and refusing to play. We need to get to the root cause and ask ourselves what is causing the anxiety and depression. One size never fits all, but you often find shame lurking in the background. Dr Heather Churchill and author Claire Musters write:

Shame is what we feel at a heart level about ourselves, and it develops through painful early experiences. The ongoing message we give ourselves is 'I am wrong, I am rubbish, I hate myself.' It is not the feeling that we have done something wrong but more a feeling that we are wrong. Shame triggers self-condemnation, self-criticism and the desire to hide.[2]

Shame operates both externally and internally. External shame is about the image we believe others have of us, Sometimes this isn't based on any evidence, but shame tells us it is real. Internal shame is about the way we perceive ourselves and the judgements we make about ourselves as a result. As we are holistic beings, shame can affect us emotionally, behaviourally, cognitively, physically and spiritually.

A number of factors can affect our shame levels. These may include some or all of the following:

- Age and gender
- Family background
- Work status
- Financial situation
- Being a parent (or not)
- Physical health
- Mental health
- Unhelpful labelling
- Body image
- Religious beliefs
- Trauma
- Compulsive behaviours
- Surviving trauma
- Being stereotyped or labelled

We all have experience in a number of these areas, because the truth is that at some point we will all suffer from shame. It's part of the human experience. The strange thing is, we rarely talk about it. Instead, we keep it secret, which only increases our sense of isolation.

We often allow our shame to tell us we are not worthy of connection or belonging, as we are flawed and unlovable. We believe it when it tells us to be quiet and keep how we're feeling to ourselves. Many of us need to begin calling out these lies and bringing them into the light.

Responses to shame

When we feel shame, our brains quickly go into flight, fight or freeze mode. The rational side of the brain (the prefrontal cortex) is taken over by the emotional side (the limbic system), which in turn affects our behaviour. These responses are there for our survival; they are inbuilt and have an important function when we're under attack. But they are not that helpful if what we need is empathy, connection and compassion.

Do any of these responses ring a bell for you?

Checking out

Shame can make us want to hide, even when we're with people we usually feel comfortable with. We might stay in the room physically, but mentally and emotionally we've checked out. We avoid people we know. We look the other way when we see someone in a crowd or pretend we're on the phone when someone is walking down the street towards us. We'll use any avoidance tactic so we don't have to engage.

Hulk-like

We become irritable and angry at the smallest thing. We take everything personally. An email or social media comment we don't like results in a swift reply (though, often, as soon as we've pressed 'send' we regret it), or a small mistake by a fellow driver on the road leaves us raging, as though they've committed a huge crime.

Approval needed

We feel like those self-service checkouts that shout 'approval needed' when we try to buy a bottle of wine. We need to find someone who approves of us, someone we can please, who will feed our sense of being. This approval can be addictive, but it's just a temporary fix. If we don't get to the bottom of how we're feeling, the validation doesn't last.

Shame voice

We make a mistake at work and feel lousy and embarrassed. The boss is fine with it, and appreciates that mistakes are part of learning and progress, yet the voice of shame shouts loudly in our heads, 'You're no good! You shouldn't have tried something new. You should know better. You're a complete failure!'

Shame vs the truth

Shame says:	*The truth says:*
You are no good.	You are more than your mistakes.
You shouldn't have tried something new.	We can't improve or be creative if we don't take any risks.
You should know better.	Why? Says who? How could you have known what would happen? You deserve credit for showing up and giving it a go.
You're a failure.	Failing at one thing does not make anyone a failure. Our self-worth is not up for grabs based on what we achieve; we are valuable regardless.

Dolphins are stressful

Growing up, I loved the TV programme *Flipper*. Flipper was a friendly dolphin who used to hang out with kids, wave at them, take them on rides and was basically a bit of a hero. I had posters of dolphins on my wall, and it became my lifetime ambition to swim with one.

A few years ago, I finally got the chance while on holiday with my family in Egypt. We got to the boat early, eager for the magical experience ahead. I couldn't have been more excited when the instructor called those of us who were getting into the water to come to the back of the boat. We lined up and the instructor gave each child a life jacket, then asked each adult in turn if they needed one. One by one they all said no, they were strong swimmers. I was the last person he asked. I am not a strong swimmer, but I couldn't bear the thought of being the weakest adult. 'I'm fine,' I said with a smile, while my heart sank.

A second later he said, 'Jump now or you'll miss them!' Everyone started jumping, and I followed my kids, who had moved without hesitation. As I landed in the water, I took a deep breath in instead of breathing out through my snorkel. I swallowed some sea water and was struggling to breathe, but I kept thinking, *I can't miss this magical moment*, so I put my head back under the water. Suddenly, three dolphins swam past at high speed, but much to my disappointment, not one of them waved or offered to take me on a ride.

When I came up to the surface, I was further away from the boat than I'd intended, and it was moving away from me. I was struggling to catch my breath and didn't have it in me to swim after it. My heart was racing as I tried to work out what to do. The obvious thing was to ask for help, but I felt too embarrassed. I tried to subtly get Diane's attention, but she thought I was waving and started filming me. I couldn't have her film her husband drowning! I had to admit defeat.

'Help!' I shouted. The instructor immediately threw me the ring of shame (a life-buoyancy ring), and I grabbed hold of it tightly, my heart still racing as I struggled to get my breathing under control. Suddenly, my son Daniel popped up next to me. 'Alright All Dad?' he said. 'Swimming with dolphins is pretty stressful, innit?'

I looked at the instructor, waiting to be told off for being stupid and not taking a life jacket. He looked me in the eye as he helped me back into the boat and said kindly, 'Breathe. You're OK. It's tough out there, but you're safe now.'

Despite his kindness, waves of shame rolled over me, and I hid myself in the privacy of the bathroom until I felt ready to face them again.

It wasn't a feeling of being embarrassed or humiliated; it was shame. The relationship between humiliation and shame is complex. Humiliation is a horrible feeling of being exposed and having nowhere to hide. The main difference between humiliation and shame is that you don't believe you deserve the feeling. But humiliation can turn into shame if you start believing its messages. My incident in the sea reinforced a negative belief that there is something fundamentally flawed about me. It served as evidence of something I was already struggling with. Someone else might have shrugged it off and not thought much of it, if they had a stronger sense of self-belief and it didn't tap into any shame triggers for them. Two people can react very differently to the same situation depending on their self-talk and their beliefs.

When I reflected on why I didn't say yes to a life jacket, I thought back to my school days. I have always been a weak swimmer, and the kids in my class laughed at me because I was one of the last people to achieve my ten-metre badge in swimming lessons. My pride got in the way of me accepting the life jacket. I didn't want my kids to think I was weaker than the other parents, and I found myself caught in the comparison trap.

I felt stupid admitting that something so small had triggered such shame, but I knew I needed to speak to Diane about what was going on inside my head. She could have laughed it off, but instead she showed me a great deal of empathy and understanding. She asked me what I would say to someone else who had been through the same experience. I realised that none of the harsh words I used towards myself would have even entered my thinking. 'Perhaps I'd say, "You are a great dad. You made yourself uncomfortable so you could share an experience with your children. Next time be wiser about your limitations, but you can be sure that the kids will never forget this day."'

This experience taught me three things about handling shame:

1 Have the courage to share your story.
2 Show yourself some compassion.
3 Rewrite the ending.

Talking to Diane changed, and I came to realise that shame tends to multiply when we keep it to ourselves and dwell on it. Diane helped me be kind to myself (asking how you would treat a loved one in the same situation is a fairly safe bet that you'll respond with kindness and encouragement), and that helped me rewrite the ending.

We don't have to stop at shame. That's not the final answer. I had wanted to hide from my family and never have this embarrassing day mentioned again. Now I can laugh at myself, and even enjoy my family teasing me. It's become a standing tradition that whenever someone in our family goes away, they bring back a dolphin magnet to put on the fridge, and we all laugh about it again.

Belonging

Psychologist Abraham Maslow is famous for defining a hierarchy of needs for human beings, and right in the middle sits 'belonging'. It is a fundamental human need – one that none of us can escape, even if we try to convince ourselves we're OK on our own. When we belong somewhere, we know we are accepted as we are – we don't feel as if we have to adapt ourselves in order to fit in. We can be ourselves.

One of the signs of belonging is that we feel free to tell our stories without shame. That's one of the goals of our Kintsugi Hope Wellbeing Groups. We want to create a space where people feel safe, connected, free from judgement and under no pressure to have it all together. People should feel valuable and loved as they are, and know that whatever their story is, it will be treated as sacred.

During lockdown, most of the Kintsugi groups moved online. Our leaders observed that some folk often had their lights turned down low, had their cameras at an angle so you couldn't see their faces properly or turned their cameras off altogether.

Anne was one of the women who didn't want to be seen. Her children had been taken into foster care after a judge decided they could no longer live with her, and the impact of the pain and anxiety on Anne's self-esteem was huge. The group discussed shame and how it is different from guilt. They looked at how you can step out of shame by owning your story, and talked about how – despite all of our mistakes – we are all still deserving of love and connection.

The following week Anne's light was on, her camera was on, and for the first time she felt able to let people see her clearly.

God's first words

Many of us think that, if God exists, he stands at the gates of heaven when we die with a disappointed look on his face and a long list in his hand of all the things we've done wrong. We imagine he'll say, 'You made a right mess of that.' 'You should have tried harder.' 'You have so much to be ashamed of.'

These images sometimes come from old TV programmes we've watched (I always remember one episode of *The Simpsons* where God appeared to Homer – long hair and white beard flowing – and accused him of abandoning the faith! Sometimes they are the voices of our parents, or they're our worst fears about ourselves made up of all the negative voices we've heard throughout our lives.

Author and mystic Brennan Manning gave me a new way of thinking about this. He says he thinks the first question God might ask us is, 'Did you believe I loved you?'[3]

Turns things on their head, doesn't it?

Affirmations

We spend a great deal of time telling ourselves things – and when our mental health is bad, these words often aren't very kind. Affirmations can provide us with true and positive words to counter these negative thought patterns. They may feel a bit silly to say at first, but in time they retrain our brains to believe the things we're saying. So, when shame shows up, talk back to it. Try one of these affirmations:

'I am worthy of love.'

'Making mistakes doesn't make me a bad person.'

'My body is strong and capable.'

'I am enough.'

Go gently

Dealing with shame is something that should be done with gentle care, although I'll admit it's taken me a while to realise that gentleness is a strength and not a weakness. Gentleness goes against the dominant culture of our time, which says that everything needs to be sorted quickly, efficiently and with minimum fuss.

I love this definition of gentleness by author and social justice activist L. R. Knost:

> Gentleness is not weakness. Just the opposite. Preserving a gentle spirit in a heartless world takes extraordinary courage, determination, and resilience. Do not underestimate the power of gentleness because gentleness is strength wrapped in peace, and therein lies the power to change the world.[4]

When we're struggling with shame, we often attack ourselves, especially when we make a mistake. Sometimes deep-rooted shame is the result of difficult childhood experiences that need to be handled with compassion and care. As well as sharing with a trusted friend, and perhaps a good social/support group, an experienced therapist is invaluable to help us step out of deeply rooted shame. It takes courage and vulnerability, because we have to take the step when we still believe we are worthy of these feelings of shame, trusting that somehow there is freedom on the other side.

Shame isn't a good motivational tool for healing or for long-term meaningful change; all of us who have ever tried to shame ourselves for the way we look to motivate us to become fitter and healthier know this is true. It never ends well. Compassion and gentleness have the strength to bring about real change.

So, go gently.

A light on the dashboard

I know very little about cars, but when a light flashes on the dashboard, even I know that something is wrong. It's a strong signal – designed so it can't be easily ignored – that tells me I need to take action. Sometimes it's a problem I can fix – a passenger needs to put their seatbelt on or I need to get some petrol – but sometimes I need to take it in for some specialist help. The light disrupts my journey, but it's telling me something important. In many ways, anger is the flashing light of our emotional toolkit.

We are often taught that anger is wrong, that it's a 'bad' emotion; one we should suppress at all costs and certainly not talk about. Really, it's just a sign, an indicator, telling us to check out what else is going on – perhaps that a need has gone unmet, a goal has been blocked, a boundary has been breached or an injustice has occurred.

In their book, *An Insight into Anger*, Wendy Bray and Chris Ledger write:

> Anger is not wrong, it's not right. It just is, like the weather, it is a fact of life. On any one day the weather can range from sunshine to downpours – often on the same day! But we wouldn't say either type of weather was wrong. One kind may be a little more pleasant or less wet than the other; more damaging or unpredictable, but neither is wrong. We just have to respond to what the weather is appropriately: bikini or umbrella! Similarly, it's how we deal with anger that can be judged right or wrong: how we express it that is appropriate or inappropriate.[1]

One of the reasons we see anger as wrong is that we associate it so strongly with violence and aggression, though they are separate things. Undealt-with anger may lead to violence, aggression and many terrifying consequences, but anger is not inherently wrong.

Most of us learn ways of dealing with or suppressing anger through the way we saw it modelled in our families. Often, we would get shut down (sent out of the room or told to be quiet), or perhaps had a parent who tried to immediately soothe the outburst or deflect from it rather than look at what was making us angry. This means that even as grown adults we don't always feel fully equipped to deal with anger, which makes it feel like a dangerous emotion. Our flight-or-fight mechanism is activated, and we can lose perspective on what's happening. Often we find that we are viewing the situation through the lens of old and unresolved pain. It's easy to lash out – sometimes at the wrong person or at the wrong time – because our anger has become misplaced or is spilling over.

We need to learn to look at the flashing red light and give ourselves a moment to think about what the problem really is and how it can best be dealt with.

Beneath the anger

Any intense emotion deserves attention to try to work out what's going on underneath, but, as we discussed in chapter 1, we often have a very limited vocabulary when it comes to describing our emotions. We might say, 'I'm angry,' when we're mildly irritated, extremely annoyed, furious or completely outraged. Pinpointing our exact feelings helps us to understand them, express them, and take healthy and appropriate action.

I asked some friends which emotions they can feel behind their anger, and they replied:

Frustration	Love
Grief	Regret
Loneliness	Hurt
Bitterness	Disappointment
Sadness	Hopelessness
Guilt	Anxiety
Shame	Fear
Betrayal	

They described feeling inadequate, overlooked, rejected or invalidated; feeling overloaded, stuck and unable to express themselves; seeing and experiencing injustice; feeling like they are not valued or appreciated, and are being misunderstood; living in fear and feeling helpless or hopeless; feeling worthless or insignificant and not fitting in; being out of control and close to burnout.

Next time you feel angry, stop and think about how many of these things apply. What's really going on?

Rhino vs hedgehog

Experts often talk about the two different ways we tend to respond when we are angry, known as the rhino and hedgehog. Do you recognise either in yourself?

Rhino	Hedgehog
I overreact and go on the attack	I fail to admit I'm angry and/or hurt
I react by becoming confrontational	I give my partner the silent treatment
I say things I later regret	I try to ignore my feelings
I demand immediate discussion of the issue	I withdraw or shut down
I bring up past hurts that are not related to the issue	I withhold physical affection

Unexpressed anger

Many of us think of anger as loud, aggressive and overt, yet it can also be passive and quiet, hidden behind a wall of silence. When we don't find a healthy way to express how we're feeling, the resentment can chip away at us and do incredible damage, even harming our health.

Psychologist Robert Firestone writes, 'Holding back angry feelings creates tension, and this stress reaction plays a part in a wide range of psychosomatic ailments, such as headaches, hypertension, cardiovascular disease, and cancer.'[2]

We sometimes see biting our tongue or holding back our anger as a helpful thing; a way to rise above the situation and try to diffuse it. In marriages and relationships where things are difficult, we assume it's better for parents to keep quiet in front of their kids. However, a study carried out by the University of Rochester in New York found that it wasn't only the overt gestures, such as swearing or throwing items across the room, that caused children distress, but also the sulking and silent treatment often used by those who feel they are doing the right thing by refusing to argue in front of their kids.[3]

Sometimes we're not angry at a person, but at a situation... and what do we do with our anger then? I found myself angrier than ever after my first knee operation. All my usual stress-relief outlets were unavailable, as I couldn't play football or have a chat with a friend and let off some steam. Instead, I was confined to the sofa in excruciating pain, tortured by the knowledge that I'd have to go through the whole thing again when they operated on the other leg. I could only lie there, helplessly, watching Diane at the end of herself in trying to take care of me and the kids. Every two hours I could take pills to keep the physical pain at bay, but there was nothing to numb the rising anger. It all felt so unjust. *Why me?* I would ask on an endless loop. *Why am I the one who got a degenerative knee condition?* I didn't want to add to Diane's burden by letting out my frustrations – she was dealing with enough – so instead I quietly seethed.

I began to imagine what it would feel like to pick up the coffee table in our lounge and throw it against the wall, or I would stare at a glass in my hand and imagine it hitting the window and shattering into tiny pieces. I started being intensely self-critical, beating myself up for every little thing and feeling worthless because I couldn't do anything to contribute to the running of our family. My perceptions of myself and of others became distorted. I imagined that everyone was cross with me: friends, family, work colleagues. I was convinced they were fed up with me.

It took a therapist to help me see that internalising my anger was fuelling low self-esteem and depression. She helped me recognise the unhelpful coping mechanisms I had picked up in the past and, that over time, I needed to explore those memories to help me rescript how I could deal with the natural anger I was feeling. I started doing exercises to imagine myself in the situations that make me feel angry and powerless. Then I would think about how they could look if a friend, or a bigger version of me, was there – a person who would give me space to express how I was feeling, to stand up for me, to make sure others in the room listened to me without judgement. It was a strangely powerful experience that I hadn't been expecting.

What happened?

Unexpressed anger can spill out at the most unusual times. I have noticed this when my own reactions to a person or a situation seem out of proportion. Things can escalate so quickly. I have also seen this time and time again when working with young people in my community.

One particular kid comes to mind, and his name is Omar. He lived on the estate I was working on in my twenties, and he hadn't had an easy life. He had seen violence in the home as well as in the community, as there had been a murder across the road from where he lived. He knew about poverty first-hand, watching his parents work day and night but never seeming to be able to change their circumstances. There is something so unjust about persistent poverty; it can leave people with a real sense of shame and embarrassment that often leads to anger. Omar had to be tough to survive.

One afternoon, a big group of us were having a snowball fight on the estate just outside the local church, when I lobbed a shot and got Omar straight in the face. Everyone laughed, and I went off to grab some more snow before I realised Omar was walking over to me. For a second, I was worried he'd been hurt and was about to ask if he was OK when I saw him pull a spanner out of his coat pocket. It wasn't unusual for the kids we worked with on the estate to carry all sorts of weapons, as they felt they needed to defend themselves on the streets, but I'd never had one pulled on me before. His face was red, his eyes fixed on me, his hand clenched at his side. My friend saw what was happening and tried to talk him into giving us the weapon, but he was having none of it. He looked completely out of control. Thankfully, my friend caught hold of him and managed to throw the spanner onto the ground before anything could happen, but it came pretty close.

I knew the kids we were working with experienced violence on a regular basis. They would pull knives on each other, throw chairs at the teachers they were arguing with, come to youth group with bruises from fighting with their friends or siblings. Anger spilled out all the time. It's easy to look at a child like Omar pulling a spanner out during a snowball fight and say, 'What is *wrong* with you? Why would you want to hurt someone who is just trying to help you?' But maybe a kinder, more insightful, question when dealing with anger would be, 'What happened to you? What trauma caused you to respond like this?'

Children aren't born angry. This isn't about offering excuses for people's behaviour and saying it doesn't matter. It does, and there are consequences to all the choices we make. Violence is not OK and we should always prioritise safety, but we also need to take time to understand that if someone is being violent it's often because they've experienced trauma in their lives. True understanding will always challenge our perspective.

'L' is for LIFESTYLE

If you hit your hand with a hammer, it's not going to help if someone gives you a list of ways you should react. You probably just need to shout or swear for a minute and wait for the pain to pass. There's a danger in pretending there's a formula we can use in any and every situation, no matter the context, but it's important for us to understand what triggers our anger and then have the courage to act on it in a healthy way. We also need to look at our lifestyle and see whether we're helping or hindering ourselves when it comes to anger.

If we're exhausted and constantly feeling overstretched, the chances are we'll get irritable and angrier much more quickly than if we're looking after our wellbeing. We tend to think of resting as doing nothing. However, looking after ourselves means we are far better able to deal with the challenges life throws at us. Looking after our wellbeing shouldn't be something on a to-do list that we fit in if we've got time; it should be a priority that allows the other areas of our lives to function at their best.

Carl Jung is often quoted as saying, 'Hurry is not just of the devil, it is the devil.' I find busyness and hurry sneak up on me. I look at my diary and realise there are no gaps. I'm trying my best to meet everyone's needs – those of my family and the people I work with and for – but what *I* need doesn't get a look in. When we live like this our margins are very thin; there's always something unexpected that crops up, which means even the tiny amount of time we thought we had is gone. Before we know it, we're exhausted and depleted, and realise that life has felt like that for the longest time.

I'd love to tell you I'm a self-help guru who is about to enable you to find your life's perfect balance in three easy steps, but, just like you, I'm still trying to figure it out. Between work, family, households to run, finances to manage, complex relationships and all the fun and games that make up everyday life, how can we find the time to look after ourselves?

Huge changes can be overwhelming, and hard to implement or sustain, but psychologists like Susan David say that small habits or tiny tweaks are much easier to maintain, and therefore make more difference in the long term.[4] So now, rather than imagining a genie is going to come along and grant me my three wishes – one of which involves a week on a secluded island with my own cook and cleaner – I look at my diary and ask: What would be the small wins for me this week? Can I find thirty minutes to exercise? Am I doing enough of the things that bring me life and make me feel good (hanging out with friends/family, getting some time to be alone, pursuing hobbies, eating well, praying and meditating) to balance out the demands that can leave me feeling drained? I try to keep these goals flexible and realistic. It's better to aim to walk for twenty minutes and do it than aim for a two-hour gym session I'll never achieve.

We can't control everything that comes our way, and we're unlikely to be able to completely eradicate anger from our lives. But we can set ourselves up to win by taking care of some of our basic needs.

Managing anger with the 4 'A's: Arousal, Appraisal, Approval, Action[5]

Arousal

What has caused the anger? What are the triggers at play here?

Why am I feeling like this? Is it caused by an old hurt or fear that's come to the surface?

Is my goal being blocked in this situation? Is my goal here realistic or unrealistic?

Am I hungry, tired or stressed?

Appraisal

Review your options and think about how you could choose to react.

Approval

Of the options you've just thought of, which reaction is justified?

Will I be pleased with the way I reacted this time next week or next year?

Action

Decide whether it's time to act or whether you need to wait until you're calmer.

For example, someone at work has been speaking negatively about you behind your back.

Arousal: There is a feeling of betrayal that touches on some bruises from the past when something similar happened at your last job. There is a blocked goal of feeling accepted at work.

Appraisal: There are two ways you can respond – a negative way and a positive way.

Negative – You could lay into that person when you're alone, bad mouth them to anyone who will listen, or give them the cold shoulder.

Positive – You could give the person the benefit of the doubt, as you're hearing the information second-hand, assuming the best of them until you have spoken directly.

Approval: You can think through these options.

Negative – 'This is justified. They deserve it; I am just giving them some of their own medicine, and maybe next time they'll keep their big mouth shut.'

Positive – 'I'll feel better about this tomorrow if I've dealt with it directly. Maybe I'll ask a colleague to be in the meeting with us so we can get to the bottom of what's going on.'

Action: 'I think I need to wait until I feel calmer before I meet with them. At the moment I'm too angry and hurt to listen to what they say, and it's likely to make the situation worse. I'm also going to chat to a friend about why this has caused a strong reaction in me, because I don't think I've dealt with the things that have happened to me in the past. I don't want to pull negativity from the past into this current situation.'

A catalyst for change

In many ways, there is truth behind the saying, 'If you're not angry, you're not paying attention. There is so much to be angry about. There's so much violence in our world, so much poverty, discrimination, injustice and inequality that we really *should* be angry. Anger can be a powerful catalyst for change. It's not about holding on to it, stewing on it, letting it lead to hatred and either verbal or physical aggression – it's about transforming and channelling it into action that brings about change.

When I was 16 I spent some of my summer holiday in London, working with an organisation called Oasis. I had been to London before with my family and we had visited all the usual sights like Big Ben and St Paul's. But this time my eyes were opened to a whole new side to the city. I'd heard of a place known as Cardboard City, near Waterloo station, where people who were experiencing homelessness congregated, but I'd never seen anything like it with my own eyes. There were around 200 people living there, with little more than cardboard boxes, old pieces of wood and dirty blankets to protect them from the elements. Many looked barely out of their teens, while others – particularly the men with their unkempt beards – looked as if they should have been in nursing homes, not living out on the street.

We started chatting to people and hearing their stories. We sat in a circle as a girl who had begged enough money to buy a single burger shared it with the rest of the group. It hit hard. I had been living in a bubble, and here, sitting with people who had no beds to sleep in, no money in their pockets, no place to wash and no clean clothes to put on, the bubble finally burst. I heard that some of those around me had nowhere else to go and, for some, living on the streets was actually preferable to the alternatives. I realised with a sickening jolt that, having lived in comfort all my life, I had been completely oblivious to the depths of pain and suffering in the world.

What I saw made me sad, yes, but it also made me angry. That anger was like a fire inside me, and I went home changed. I couldn't stop thinking about the people I had met and the lives they were living. I couldn't stand it; it was so unjust. Life had been so unfair to the people living on the streets. Under a different set of circumstances, that could easily have been me sleeping in a cardboard box. But I didn't simply want to stay angry at the injustices of the world; I wanted to channel that anger into positive energy to make a difference.

When I left school, I headed straight back to London for a gap year, which gave me an opportunity to work on a south London estate. After a pupil at my local school was stabbed in the school playground, I decided to start a charity called XLP to work with young people and their families living in some of the most financially deprived areas. We longed to have a sustainable impact on poverty and educational failure.

When I look back, I can see how much that sense of anger at the injustices I saw – and continue to see – caused me to act. Without that anger, without the fire it lit for change, I'm not sure either XLP or Kintsugi Hope would have even begun.

'Anger rages' by Terry Waite

Anger rages
Like a consuming fire,
Destroying all
That would impede
Its relentless pathway.

Do not extinguish
The flames totally.
Calm them.
And warm yourself
By the gentle glow
Of the embers.

From *Out of the Silence*[6]

Being human

Grief and loss are part of the human experience; there's no escaping that. If we hope, we can be disappointed. If we gain something, we've got something to lose. If we love, we will grieve. Sometimes grief is subtle; the dull and nagging ache of loss and change. Sometimes grief is blindsiding; slicing our lives into 'before' and 'after'. Even when something positive happens – kids grow up and leave home or we leave an old job for a new one – there's usually loss around it. We don't grieve all losses equally, but none of us can escape grief. It's a package deal that comes with being alive.

I experienced loss early in my life with my younger brother dying the day before my third birthday. As an adult, my losses have been varied: my wife had a miscarriage, and moving on to start Kintsugi Hope meant saying goodbye to XLP – a charity I had founded and run for more than twenty-two years. As a I write this, I am freshly grieving my dear uncle who died at the age of sixty-four, as well as a friend of mine who was only forty-seven. Different memories, different ways they impacted my life, but both heartbreaking.

I'm not an expert on grief, but I've learned some things the hard way. With my younger brother, I knew the pain had been much harder on my parents than it was on me, so as I grew up I tried to hide how I felt. I thought their grief was more important than mine, so I didn't validate how I felt or give myself permission to grieve. It didn't work, and it all caught up with me in my teenage years. When Diane had a miscarriage, I tried to bottle up my emotions again. As she was the one who had carried our baby, I thought I should 'be strong' by not crying. Unsurprisingly, that didn't work either. Now I'm learning that there's strength in being honest about the pain we're going through.

Grief is uncomfortable. We want to find a way around it, and many people in our lives will encourage us to do so. 'Don't cry,' they say, 'it's OK' – when it's clearly anything but. We don't need to hide our feelings or gloss over the pain with awful clichés; we need to validate how we feel and know that it's OK to be confused, frustrated, angry, sad or numb. Being honest with ourselves and others is more important than everyone feeling comfortable. There's strength in crying, in taking time to grieve and in asking for help when we need it. I'm learning this myself; I've booked in some time to talk through my grief with someone I trust next week.

You have permission to grieve...

- The loss of someone you cared about, even if someone else was closer to them.
- The end of a dream.
- How things could have been.
- Friendships that have changed or been lost.
- Your parents divorcing, even when you're an adult.
- A relationship, even when you were the one who ended it.
- The home you loved.
- Your independence.
- A change in your identity.
- The loss of a pet.
- The loss of your physical health.
- The death of a famous person you never met, but who impacted your life regardless.

The lies we tell about grief (things not to say to someone who is grieving!)

'Time heals all wounds.'
Grief may change over time, but it rarely disappears completely.

'God must have wanted another angel.'
God is not a twisted puppeteer plucking people off to be his angels.

'Only the good die young.'
The good, like the bad, can die at any age.

'Everything happens for a reason.'
Trying to find a reason for a painful loss can lead us into really unhelpful thought patterns. Sometimes there is no 'why'.

'It was God's will.'
Even for those who believe in God, this is a hugely unhelpful statement that can lead to us blaming God rather than finding comfort in him.

'I know just how you feel.'
No one grieves in the same way as someone else. Even if you've both been through the same loss – e.g., both have lost a spouse, a parent or a child – our relationships are different, so none of us can know exactly how someone else is feeling. Human beings are more complex than that.

'You just need to be strong.'
Usually what we mean here is that we want someone to stop showing emotion. That's not strength; that's suppression. Feeling our feelings and expressing them is strength.

'You'll get over it.'
We don't 'get over' grief; it shapes and changes us. That doesn't mean it will always hurt with the same ferocity, but to say we'll 'come out the other side' isn't usually helpful.

Ambiguous losses

When a person we love dies, there is usually a set of rituals we go through. We have to let people know what has happened, we arrange a funeral, we have the worst heap of admin ('death-min') to deal with. Likewise, when someone we know loses a loved one, we are primed to send flowers, attend the funeral and make the family food in those early days when they can't think straight.

But some losses do not have these clear processes. They don't start on one specific day. Rather, they are losses that happen over a period of time with no definitive markings. This type of loss hasn't often been talked about, but it's become known as 'ambiguous loss' – a loss that is uncertain or unknown, often with no resolution and therefore no closure. It might be that someone we love is deeply impacted by an addiction. We hope that one day they will be free, but we live in the uncertainty of whether or not there will be change. Something similar happens if a loved one is in a coma, goes missing, has a chronic mental illness, suffers a stroke or has a disease like Alzheimer's, as my precious Nan did.

One friend of mine longed to have children all of her adult life but remained single. Because she couldn't actively try for a baby, there was no obvious point to hinge her hopes on and no clear-cut journey for how to get where she wanted to be, or to know if it would ever happen. There was no medical support, and there were no investigations doctors could do to help her see if her dream would become a reality; just a long wait to see if she might meet someone she would want to start a family with. She said, 'There were no landmarks or defined moments of grief, which made it really hard to process. Some days the pain was overwhelming and I'd find myself completely broken. Other days I was full of hope that it wouldn't be too long until my dream would be fulfilled.'

Though she was honest with close friends, to the rest of the world there was no visible pain or grief, which meant she was often subjected to difficult and intrusive questions. There wasn't a key moment when people could rally around and comfort her in her grief. She said:

> I can only imagine the agony people go through when they're told they can't have children for medical reasons, but in some ways I wished I could have been given that clarity. If I knew I would never be a mum, it would have been awful, but it felt like living in limbo was its own special hell. With a definitive answer, I would have been forced to let go and move on, to grieve fully and then decide what life was going to look like.

She says it was a slow realisation in her forties that it wasn't going to happen:

> Other than waiting for my body to be biologically incapable of pregnancy, I had to choose the moment to let go of the grief it was causing me to hold on to the dream. Friends often wanted to offer hope that it would still happen; they were trying to be kind because they knew how much I longed for a family of my own. But I got to a point where I knew I was the only one who could decide when enough was enough. I'd grieved so much over the years that when I reached the place of accepting it wasn't going to happen, there was a sense of peace that came, even within the pain.

Her story is a reminder to me of the losses people deal with every day; the ones you can't always see and that society doesn't make space to talk about. It reminds me why people say that we should always be kind because everyone we meet is fighting a battle we are completely unaware of.

Handling grief – in five easy steps?

Many years ago, Elisabeth Kübler-Ross, a Swiss-American psychiatrist, pioneer in near-death studies and author of the groundbreaking book *On Death and Dying* (Taylor & Francis, 1969), identified five stages of grief. Ever since, people have been trying to turn her many years of research into an easy formula, desperately trying to find a neat and tidy process to help us in our grief. But grief isn't neat and tidy; it's wild, messy and raw. That doesn't mean the research isn't incredibly helpful. It is.

Kübler-Ross identified these five stages:

- Denial
- Anger
- Bargaining
- Depression
- Acceptance

When I first heard about these stages, I assumed I would journey through them, one by one, until I arrived at acceptance, when I would be fine and whole. What a nice idea. But I kept getting stuck in phases or feeling like I was going backwards, circling back to the same things. I'd be depressed one day and angry the next, and then I'd get frustrated with myself for not being where I thought I should be. It turns out we can't tackle grief as though it's a project on a deadline. We can't just 'be proactive', get our heads down and get through – reaching a magical 'other side' when we've put in enough time or energy.

Tanya Marlow is an author and speaker I admire hugely. She has had ME for more than a decade, and is only able to get out of bed for a few hours each day. Tanya pointed out to me that Kübler-Ross's stages of grief were actually what she had witnessed in those who were dying, not those left behind when a loved one dies. Tanya said,

'Other grief is messier, it comes in bursts. It has its own timetable and doesn't fit with what we want it to do. We want to plough a line through grief, but it's more like surfing. You've just got to keep afloat.'

Grief isn't an emotion we cycle through; it's something that changes us at a profound level. When we've loved and lost, we'll never be the same... and neither should we want to be.

A ball in a box

Imagine your grief as a ball in a box.

Inside the box there is also a pain button. When you first experience a deep grief, the ball may feel so large that you can barely move or function without it hitting the pain button. Many of us know this feeling from those early weeks and months after a devastating loss. You can think of little else, and doing normal, everyday activities you previously took for granted suddenly feels like climbing a mountain. It feels as though the pain will never change; it will always be there, consuming your every waking moment.

Over time, the ball seems to shrink a little. It is by no means gone, and every time it hits the pain button the agony is intense, but you can function a little more and the pain isn't as consistent. As more time passes, the ball gets smaller and the times of pain are less frequent again. They may still have the power to take our breath away, but there is more time to recover in between each hit. For most of us, the ball and the pain never disappear completely, and we carry elements of grief around with us throughout our lives.

This illustration helped me see that instead of thinking of grief as something I could work through and come out the other side of, my grief would change over time. Then, rather than beating myself up for not having 'got over it' when I felt the intensity of loss, I realised I just needed to be gentle with myself.

Some people find it more helpful to imagine that the grief stays as large as it did in the early days of loss, but the box gets bigger. In other words, life grows around our grief, as our days and weeks become filled with other experiences.

Whichever illustration is the most helpful to you, I hope it's a comforting reminder that we need to be kind to ourselves. Some days will be hard and that's OK; others we might laugh and feel happy, and that's OK too. Grief will look different on different days, and we're not doing it right or wrong. There is no such thing.

Exercises that might help

Try writing in a journal

Journals can be great places to write unfiltered. When speaking to friends or family, we sometimes worry we're talking for too long, repeating ourselves or being negative. In a journal we are free to express ourselves without filters, without trying to find an upside to our loss, and without putting on a brave face. Don't feel like you have to make sense or write beautiful prose; no one is grading this – it's just for your benefit. Likewise, write for however long suits you. As little as a few minutes can make a difference, but you might find it's so helpful that you write for longer. Give yourself some space before you go back to everyday life after writing, it can bring up some raw emotions and you don't want to have to rush.

Try writing a psalm

A psalm is a sacred song or poem used in worship. It can be a great way to release all of our questions, difficult feelings and painful emotions. You may choose to end the psalm with some more positives – perhaps things you're grateful for about the person or situation you've lost, or you may just want to write down the hard things.

Name your emotions

We can't deal with our emotions if we can't name them. Get specific. Do you feel sadness, guilt, fear, anger, betrayal, worry, numbness, gratitude, regret, jealousy, overwhelm, dread, resignation, relief, resentment and/or calmness? Name as many emotions as you can.

Tell your story

Speak to safe people and share your experience. Talking helps!

Support

There are support groups for many types of grief, and having peers who are experiencing something similar to us can offer great comfort. These can be places where we are able to share our feelings without worrying about being a burden or being judged. Many who attend these groups say they make them feel less lonely, give them a safe space to be honest, improve their coping skills and help to restore hope.

Chasing rabbits

There's nothing our dog Hope likes more than a walk – well, maybe there is one thing: the rabbits she encounters along the way! She's so excitable she strains against the lead until we get to a field where she can be let off and go in search of the gold at the end of her rainbow. We've been doing this for years, and she runs and runs and runs until she's completely exhausted. To this day, she has never caught a rabbit. Silly dog.

But don't we all chase the perfect life, the perfect relationship, the perfect body? Our goal may be completely unattainable, but it doesn't stop us striving to achieve it, causing us to run ourselves ragged in the process. Perfectionism is a moving target we will never hit; a rabbit we will never catch.

Growing up, I thought perfectionism only applied to kids whose parents put too much pressure on them to get good grades at school. My parents never did that, so I figured it was not an issue I had to deal with. It wasn't until a few years ago, when I was doing some research on perfectionism for a talk, that I had a light-bulb moment. I had completely misunderstood what perfectionism was and where it came from, and had unwittingly allowed it into my life unchallenged. I was always asking myself:

Am I good enough?
Is there something wrong with me?
How can I earn people's approval so they will accept me?
How can I push myself harder?
How can I do better? Be better?

I felt like I needed to strive, to keep pushing myself, believing the lie that 'I am what I can accomplish'. I was always worried about what others thought of me, and I didn't want to risk upsetting anyone. Underneath all these questions was perfectionism and shame.

At school I was very good at sports and hoped to become a semi-professional football player. I played for Colchester United and was being scouted by some bigger clubs, so every game I played up to the age of eighteen was closely watched. I came off the pitch analysing every aspect of my performance, always looking for ways to improve. I had never been academic, so I thought my only chance at success was to play sport at a high level. I would lie in bed the night after a game going through all the chances I had missed and the ways I could do better. I was devastated when I realised I was never going to be accepted into a professional club. I didn't feel like I was good at anything else, so what would I do with my life?

The feeling of not being enough to succeed was never far from my mind. In order to try to be enough, I worked hard to make others happy, which crept into most areas of my life, including trying to keep God happy.

I was brought up going to church, and I thought what God most wanted from me was good behaviour. It seemed the important parts of being a Christian were that I didn't swear, didn't watch anything naughty on TV and didn't ask questions that sounded like I was disagreeing with the church leaders. I was used to going to church up to three times each Sunday, but when it clashed with football when I was a teenager, the game won. It was the right decision for me, but I felt like I had really disappointed God. I was scared stiff of going to hell, as that was the most frightening thing I had ever heard of, and I felt like it was my job to warn all my friends about this terrible place so they could also escape it. I thought I had to behave in certain ways to earn acceptance from God. if I wasn't perfect, I wasn't good enough.

Brené Brown's teachings helped me understand that perfectionism is a continuum we can travel up and down at different points in our lives. She also helped me move to a healthier place on the continuum. In *Atlas of the Heart*, she writes:

Understanding the difference between healthy striving and perfectionism is critical to laying down the shield and picking up your life. Research shows that perfectionism hampers success. In fact, it often sets you on the path to depression, anxiety, addiction, and life paralysis. 'Life paralysis' refers to all of the opportunities we miss because we're too afraid to put anything out in the world that could be imperfect. It's also all of the dreams that we don't follow because of our deep fear of failing, making mistakes, and disappointing others. It's terrifying to risk when you're a perfectionist; your self-worth is on the line.[1]

I don't want to constantly have my self-worth on the line. It's exhausting never wanting to let my guard down. One of the biggest risks to our mental and emotional wellbeing is not being ourselves. We have to give ourselves permission to be who we are, and that means getting a firm handle on where we find ourselves on the perfection spectrum.

Perfectionism involves...

- **Catastrophic thinking.** The smallest argument with your partner spells the end of your relationship. You make a mistake at work and think you'll get fired. The kids get angry with you and you feel you're the worst parent in the world.

- **Mind reading.** This is linked to catastrophic thinking. We think we know what others think of us, but our assumptions are based on very little evidence and are rarely positive.

- **Unrealistic expectations.** We think we're failures for not being able to achieve the impossible – putting expectations on ourselves we would never put on others.

- **A rigid belief systems.** We use words like 'I *should*, I *must*, I *ought*,' constantly feeling like we're not measuring up. There is very little flexibility in our thinking, and if we miss our self-imposed targets, we feel terrible.

- **A hatred of making mistakes.** Making mistakes is inevitable; it's part of life. Yet rather than seeing them as being human or a necessary step towards achievement, the mistakes eat away at us, leaving us frustrated.

- **Overcompensating.** We work really hard to get everything right, overcompensating in our behaviour and pushing ourselves to the limit.

- **Excessive checking.** We don't want to let people down or offend anyone, so will comb over emails and texts before pressing 'send'. At work, we constantly look for reassurance that our ideas aren't rubbish.

- **Overcautious decision-making.** We don't want to get a decision wrong, so we procrastinate. Even small decisions are hard. Have you ever spent ages flicking through all the options on Netflix, only to have your family shout, 'Just choose a film – *any* film – we don't care any more'? (No? Just me, then.)

- **Difficulties in receiving feedback.** Perfectionists find feedback very hard to hear, whether it's positive or negative. If we hear ten positive comments and one negative, we focus in on the one negative. As a result, we fail to celebrate our achievements.

- **People-pleasing.** When we're trying to have perfect relationships, we will try to avoid saying anything that will rock the boat. We hate upsetting people, so before talking to them about something tricky, we rehearse the conversation in our head. We can also take it too personally when someone challenges us, even though we know that disagreement can be a healthy and important part of any relationship. When we become too focused on pleasing others, we start to act differently around people, which means we don't allow them to see our authentic self.[2]

Trying your best   vs   Perfectionism

Trying your best	Perfectionism
Sets attainable goals	Sets standards beyond their reach or reason
Is content with progress	Is never satisfied
Loves a challenge	Is hypervigilant
Sets self up for growth	Feels self-worth is on the line
Has normal levels of anxiety	Has a deep fear of failure
Doesn't take offence quickly	Takes criticism too personally
Uses healthy self-talk	Is self-critical
Feels energised	Feels exhausted
Is a team player	Fails to delegate
Sees mistakes as opportunities for growth	Is a people-pleaser
Is innovative	Destroys creativity

Giraffes can't dance

One of the people who has taught me the most about success is my daughter, Abigail. When she was very young she was diagnosed with a condition called nystagmus, which means she only has about 40 per cent vision and her eyes make repetitive, uncontrolled movements. These movements affect her balance and coordination, so she regularly bangs into things and knocks stuff over. All these things have, of course, been frustrating for her over the years, and she's found it hard that she can't see as well as the people around her. She has spent years attending various medical appointments, and in addition to her nystagmus, she has special complex needs.

Abigail has never come top of her class. She has never been given the part she wanted in the school assembly. Though she tries hard in school, she can't even get the 100 per cent attendance certificate because hospital appointments are regularly scheduled during school hours. Yet, she regularly gets an A for effort in her school reports. From a young age she has shown a remarkable depth of kindness and empathy – the kind you rarely see in mature adults, let alone small children. She is a generous, thoughtful and beautiful soul, always looking out for others. She makes my heart sing. I'm not pretending she's an angel, of course, but she's my precious daughter, and while I would make life easier for her in a heartbeat if I could, I love her exactly as she is. I don't want her to be anything other than my Abigail.

I first shared this story in my book *Honesty Over Silence* (Waverley Abbey Trust, 2018) but it feels appropriate to share it with you now, too. One night when Abigail was younger, Diane was reading her the book *Giraffes Can't Dance* (Orchard Books, 2014). It's about a giraffe called Gerald who lives in the jungle and gets laughed at when he goes to the annual dance because everyone knows giraffes can't dance. A despondent Gerald starts walking home and meets a cricket (as you do) who encourages him to dance, saying he should try it with different music. In the manner of all good children's books, it works, and Gerald becomes the best dancer in the jungle!

Diane closed the book, thinking it had been a nice story, and then realised Abigail's face was shining. 'It's about me!' she said excitedly. Diane asked what she meant, and Abigail replied, 'People think I can't do lots of things that I can. I just need to find a different way to do it.' It was a very special moment for us all.

An alternative voice (things to remind myself of)

- Nobody is perfect.

- All I can do is my best.

- It's OK to not always be OK.

- Making a mistake doesn't make me a failure.

- I am only human, just like everyone else.

- It's OK if some people don't like me – no one is liked by everyone.

- Everybody has bad days.

- Perfectionism and trying my best are two very different things.

Embracing brokenness

There have been two points in my life when I felt like I hit rock bottom. The first was during the long recovery from my surgeries, and the second was when I left the charity I had set up, and poured my heart and soul into for twenty-two years.

In both cases I felt completely broken. Life had not gone to plan; my prayers had not been answered the way I wanted. I was frustrated, confused, and physically, emotionally, mentally and spiritually exhausted. Both times I was forced to completely stop, and that led to me asking myself some big questions about who I was. Those questions helped me realise what a driving force perfectionism was in my life, and that it drove so many of my other unhelpful behaviours and thought patterns.

For those of us who are employed, work often becomes a massive part of our lives. But while my work has been incredibly important to me, I know that who I am is even more important. My perfectionism was making me live in fear that I wasn't enough, and that one day I would be exposed and people would realise I wasn't up to the job. The only antidote was to practise authenticity; to show up and be me – just as I am, flaws and all – and hope that I would be accepted, despite not being perfect. I also knew I needed to have the courage to face the parts of me that were very damaged. (It's easy and so very tempting to hide them away and try our best to ignore them, isn't it?) Many call those untamed emotions and wrong motives our 'shadow side' – something we'll look at in more detail when we talk about self-acceptance.

Social justice activist Bryan Stevenson said:

Embracing our brokenness creates a need and desire for mercy, and perhaps a corresponding need to show mercy. When you experience mercy, you learn things that are hard to learn otherwise. You see things you can't otherwise see; you hear things you can't otherwise hear. You begin to recognize the humanity that resides in each of us.[3]

We all feel a bit broken at times, and that's OK.

In all of this, the image of Kintsugi became so important to me. When you feel broken, smashed to pieces and unable to look at yourself in the mirror, is it possible to be restored? For your scars to be redeemed?

When everything is stripped back, we start to realise that what is really important is our ability to give and receive love. We can learn to let go of the negative voices we have picked up over the years, the constant need for affirmation from others to prove we're good enough, and the unhelpful thinking patterns. When our emotional tanks have run dry, we need to be reminded that we are loved, valued and have a purpose.

When we learn to embrace our brokenness rather than trying to hide from it, we can find it produces a humility in us because we're no longer pretending to have all the answers.

Antidotes to perfectionism

Being accepted by friends and family

Sometimes perfectionism can tell us we need to be liked and valued by all people, whereas there is real beauty in being truly known by just one person. Can you bring that person to mind? If not, who might you be able to intentionally open up to, moving forwards?

Understanding grace

Grace is an overused word, which is essentially defined as unmerited favour; a gift we didn't and could never earn, but is freely given to us anyway. At its best it means we can allow others and ourselves to make mistakes.

Having the right view of success

Success isn't about how much money you earn, or how high you climb up the career ladder; it's about being your authentic self. Aim less for perfection and more for being yourself.

Living by your values

Our values shape how we behave, think and feel. They show us our priorities and what is important to us. One of my values is family, so that means, for example, that I have to put boundaries around my work to be able to prioritise time with my kids.

Reframing the story you tell yourself when you perceive something has gone wrong

Are you telling yourself the whole story, or is there a part missing? What evidence do you have for this story? Could there be an alternate one to replace it with?

Finding a lesson in the mistake

Some of life's biggest lessons come through mistakes. Look at what you can learn rather than what you think you failed to achieve. What lessons have you learned recently?

Letting go of comparison

You are unique. Learn to appreciate the differences between yourself and your friends and family, and remember that you are not in competition with one another.

Humility

Let go of the burden that you have to know the answer to everything and always be right. It keeps us grounded to know that we will always be learning.

Reframing

Consider some situations in your life where you feel you have failed or made mistakes. Write a few of them down, then next to them write down the things they have taught you. How do you feel as you reflect on those lessons?

_____

_____

_____

_____

Take some time to think about things that feel like successes in your life and the lessons you have learned from those. How do the two lists of lessons compare?

_____

_____

_____

_____

What would it look like if you expected 10 per cent less from yourself in every area of your life? Instead of aiming for 'perfect', what would more realistic goals look like for you in your work, your relationships, your parenting and other areas of responsibility?

_____

_____

_____

_____

Perfect days

Christmas, birthdays, holidays… there are so many days that have a huge amount of pressure piled on them with the expectation that they should be perfect. I'm guessing yours go to plan as often as mine do.

One particularly memorable Christmas Day during my childhood, the cat jumped up onto the counter where the perfectly cooked turkey was resting, waiting to be carved. The turkey went flying across the floor and my poor mum ended up in tears. There was also the birthday when my mum ordered a very expensive cake from a bakery as a special treat. While we were out of the house for a few hours, the dog managed to eat half the cake and leave the other half smeared across every room in the house.

I've definitely been guilty of wanting Christmas to be perfect, so, in a bid to conquer my inner perfectionist, I made up some new rules:

- I will not try to be all things to all people.
- I will schedule in some time to rest.
- I will take things one day at a time and not push myself to the limit.
- I will accept that Christmas does not have to be perfect to be good.
- I will try to resist comparing my life to other people's social media highlights.
- I will try to stay out of debt.
- I will meditate on the Christmas story.
- Each evening I will light a candle and know that, no matter what I go through, there is still hope.

Which special events hold a perfectionist trigger for you? What rules can you write for yourself here to help you not overlook the good times in 'chasing the rabbits' of perfection?

_____

_____

_____

_____

_____

_____

Gratitude jar

A common thing perfectionists tell themselves is, 'I will be happy when this task is done... when I've mastered this skill... when I've improved at that... when I've got this...' But we never get there. There's always another task to do, another area to improve in, another thing to want. Perfection eludes us, and it means we rarely stop to celebrate all we've done and all we have.

When I have looked at the most content people I know and asked myself what they have in common, the answer is that they are deeply grateful people. I have travelled to some of the poorest countries on earth and seen people living in conditions that most of us would deem unbearable, yet they are thankful. They're not seeking perfection; they are glad for all they have, even if it's a football made out of leaves to play with, like I saw in the Asante Akim District in Ghana. I don't say that to make you feel guilty, but to inspire you with their joy. Life doesn't have to be perfect to be good! In Ghana they weren't pretending that life was easy, and I'm sure they'd have gladly taken a leather football if we'd had one to give them, but they chose to focus on what was good rather than what was missing. They recognised that even in the toughest moments they could find things to be grateful for.

Gratitude can sound fluffy, yet it's anything but. True gratitude requires grit and determination, and has nothing to do with a fuzzy feeling. I love psychologist Karen Reivich's definition of gratitude: 'hunting the good stuff'.[4] No matter how difficult our circumstances or how challenging we're finding things, we can always seek things to be grateful for. Gratitude is key to tackling perfectionism. Research shows that it can rewire our brains and block toxic emotions such as resentment, as well as producing dopamine and serotonin, the hormones that help us feel happier.

For gratitude to become part of our lives, we need to do two things that perfectionists struggle with: slow down and celebrate often.

Recently, my team and I organised a large conference, and throughout the day I rushed from one thing to another. My boss (our Chair of Trustees) got hold of me and said, 'Just take thirty seconds to look around and see how well this is going. Look at the number of people having deep conversations; feel the lovely atmosphere in the room.' My temptation is to worry about the things that could have been better, to rush off to the next thing and never to take a deep breath, see the good and celebrate it.

It's easy to focus on what's wrong – in ourselves, in others and in our world. Sometimes we can forget that there is good, especially if we spend too much time looking at the media. But all around us are people who are kind, resilient, passionate, compassionate, loyal, hardworking and self-sacrificing. I am grateful to know so many of these people. Why not have a think about the people you're grateful for, and maybe drop them a text and tell them why you appreciate them? You might be surprised how much it means to them and how much you already have – right here, right now – to celebrate.

Snake bites

Ray and Vi's son Chris died a hideous death. He was on a night out with his brother, Philip, and a friend when they were attacked by a gang of fourteen teenagers. They kicked and punched Chris until he was on the ground, then they stamped on his head and left him in a heap on a four-lane A-road. Philip had been knocked unconscious by the gang, and when he came round he saw his brother being hit by a car, which then dragged him along the road.

Chris died in hospital a few hours later. Ray and Vi weren't allowed to touch or hold him to say goodbye, as his body was considered a crime scene, and they had to wait sixteen weeks before his body was released for a funeral. None of us would blame them if they had never considered forgiveness, especially when those who appeared in court for the crime were laughing and joking as though they had no cares in the world. Even the police said they shouldn't mention forgiveness, as it could damage the legal case.

Forgiveness is hard. Vi said she was in turmoil, believing that forgiveness was the right thing to do but not wanting to do it or knowing how she could. What Ray and Vi began to realise was that unforgiveness was hard too. Vi described it as holding on to a glass of poison that was destroying her but not knowing how to let go of it. Ray said that forgiveness for him came when he realised, 'They took Christopher's life; they're not taking ours.' Ray and Vi speak of a South African saying: 'If a snake bites you, don't kill the snake; go and get help.'

Sometimes it can feel like unforgiveness protects us, but no matter how valid our anger and hate are, they ultimately cause us pain and damage. Forgiving someone can be a huge relief to the person on the receiving end, but that's not actually the point. First and foremost, forgiveness is a gift to the forgiver.

Most of us aren't dealing with the level of pain and trauma that Ray and Vi had to, but we can still learn from their response. I (like most people) find forgiveness difficult. Whenever I've been hurt, I tend to replay the situation over and over in my head like a song on a loop that won't stop, no matter how hard I try. Going over and over it never makes it easier; it just brings up more questions, more pain and more anger, as I think about how I've been wronged. I've often resisted the idea of forgiveness, thinking it meant I was letting the other person off the hook when I wanted them to take responsibility for their actions. When I think of Ray and Vi, and other parents in similar situations who have forgiven the people who took their precious child's life, I am humbled. By withholding forgiveness they couldn't have changed what happened; nothing could bring their child back. But they chose, in the midst of their pain, to forgive and set themselves free.

Forgiveness is not...

- Forgetting
- Saying that what happened to you was right
- Saying that what happened to you was your fault
- Letting someone off the hook
- Agreeing to trust the person or people who hurt you
- Giving permission for someone to continue to hurt you
- A one-off decision (sometimes you have to forgive someone for the same offence over and over)
- A feeling
- Saying that you like the person who hurt you
- Saying that you want to be in contact with the person who caused you harm
- Saying that there are no consequences for someone's actions

The impact of trauma

A word of caution about forgiveness. Sometimes we're tapping into deeply traumatic pain, and we must tread carefully. We can't tell someone they have to forgive someone else; it doesn't work like that.

In *What Happened to You?* Oprah Winfrey discusses the impact of trauma and adversity with renowned brain development and trauma expert Dr Bruce Perry. Perry explains:

> Trauma permeates all aspects of life; it echoes through the generations, across families, communities, institutions, cultures, and societies, and it does so in very complex ways. Trauma can impact our genes, white blood cells, heart, gut, lungs, and brain, our thinking, feeling, behaving, parenting, teaching, coaching, consuming, creating, prescribing, arresting, sentencing. I could go on.[1]

Trauma triggers the fight, flight or freeze response in our brains. When there are traumatic events in childhood we often freeze, as we cannot, or do not, have the capacity to fight or flee, and this can lead to trauma being internalised and buried for many years. Facing trauma can be overwhelming, especially if you feel someone is pressurising you to forgive a person or people who have hurt you. Trauma must be processed in a safe place with a safe person. This can be a long journey, often uncovering things we've suppressed for so long that we've forgotten all about them. But with the right support, with understanding and compassion, we can take steps forward and move towards freedom.

Prisoners

Ever thought you'd wait until someone has changed before you would forgive them? Decided that you can't do it unless they come to you and show you that they know how wrong they were?

Psychotherapist Nancy Colier writes:

When we need someone else to change in order for us to be OK, we are a prisoner. In the absence of forgiveness, we're shackled to anger and resentment, uncomfortably comfortable in our misbelief that non-forgiveness rights the wrongs of the past and keeps the other on the hook. And, that by holding onto that hook, there's still hope that we might get the empathy we crave, and the past might somehow feel OK. When our attention is focused outward, on getting the other to give us something, so that we can feel peace, we're effectively bleeding out not only our own power, but also our capacity for self-compassion.[2]

We need to show ourselves the care and compassion we wish someone else would, and to make looking after our hearts our priority. If we can't change someone else's attitude, we can't make our happiness dependent on it. Ultimately, we deserve something far better than being in a prison of unforgiveness: the freedom that comes from letting it go.

Benefits of forgiveness

Forgiving others can bring release and prevent us from becoming bitter. The benefits include:

- Better self-esteem
- Better relationships
- Better heart health
- Better mental health
- Better immunity against illnesses
- Lower blood pressure
- Lower levels of stress, anxiety and depression

REACH

Psychologist Everett Worthington has spent many years studying forgiveness, and he came up with the REACH[3] model to help us explore forgiving someone. Though our emotions can't be expected to adhere to a formula, I've found this a helpful exercise.

R – Recall

If we're going to let go of something that's hurt us, we have to first acknowledge that it has. We sometimes try to pretend we're not upset. Maybe it hurts our pride to admit we've been wounded or we feel like it's silly to get upset about that particular thing. Regardless, the first step is to recall the thing that hurt us and decide to choose to forgive.

E – Empathise

In non-violent or traumatic situations, put yourself in the other person's position. Think about why they might have done what they did and how they may be feeling. (There's an additional exercise on 'changing perspective' on p. 132 to explore this further.)

A – Altruistic gift

Offering forgiveness can be an act of altruism when you expect nothing in return. We've all been on the end of someone else's forgiveness and appreciated that person's grace. Extending it to someone else can be a gift to them.

C – Commit

Worthington suggests that writing a simple note to say, 'Today I forgive X for hurting me,' can help your decision to last.

H – Hold on

Rereading the notes of commitment we've written can help us to keep holding on and remind us we have made the decision to forgive.

Forgiving Grandad

My mum was one of three children and had a very difficult upbringing, as her father was a violent man. He couldn't hold down a job and would spend what little money he had on drink. One wrong look and he would throw things against the wall or even at my nan. My mum was twelve when he beat my nan so badly that she ended up in hospital – too frightened to tell the police what had happened. He was in and out of prison, mainly for stealing, and my mum was forced to visit him and sneak him cigarettes while the guards weren't looking. He had lots of affairs, but my nan stayed with him. In those days there was a real stigma attached to divorce, as well as prohibitive practicalities.

Eventually, she couldn't take it any more and took a restraining order out on him. It was a relief to them all that he was no longer around, but it forced them into poverty. They had no soap to wash with, and all they could afford to eat each night were chips. They bought clothes at jumble sales, and Mum had only one pair of knickers – which were washed once a week. With my nan out at work trying to make ends meet, Mum would often look after my uncle, who was in and out of hospital with severe asthma.

Over the years there was no contact between my mum and her dad, and she tried to blank out as much of her past as she could because it was so painful. For twenty-seven years she didn't know if he was dead or alive. When I was sixteen, he phoned Mum out of the blue, saying he'd had a stroke and would like to see the family. We all visited him at his small home. My mum and dad, my nan, my two uncles and their wives squeezed in – and the atmosphere was extremely tense. I didn't know the ins and outs of what had happened, but I did know this man had hurt my mum, so I hated him with a passion. We found out he'd had more children, so it was very strange trying to work out who everyone was and how they were related to one another.

As we were about to leave, my dad asked if we could pray together. My grandad was not a man of faith, but he said he was happy with someone else praying, so my dad began. When he finished, my mum walked across the room, looked her dad square in the eyes and said, 'Dad, no matter what you have done, I forgive you.' I couldn't understand what was happening. I knew faith was important to my parents, but this was a different level from anything I'd ever seen. All these years on I still feel emotional when I think about that moment.

Around my neck was a medal I had won in a football tournament in Germany, where I had been voted Player of the Week. Something compelled me to take it off and give it to him. My mum says it was the first time in her life she had seen him cry. As a child I hadn't made the connection that he would associate medals with the war and honours being given, and it held a deep significance for him. My mum later explained that Grandad had seen such traumatic things during the Second World War that he was never the same afterwards. As with the vast majority of those who were involved in the war, the trauma he had experienced was never processed properly.[4] He was a violent, angry and abusive man, but, as we know, that's never the full story of who someone is or why they are the way they are.

We saw him a handful of times before we received a phone call to say that he had passed away. My mum not only attended the funeral but spoke at it too, honouring her dad for giving her life. She had every right to be angry after her traumatic and frightening childhood, yet she was willing to forgive and let go of her anger.

The process of healing can take years when the hurt is deep, and forgiveness is often a choice we have to make repeatedly. I was amazed by the depth of courage it took for her to forgive him, and I'm so grateful that she didn't allow the anger and bitterness of her childhood to take root in her character, as she wouldn't have been able to be the loving, generous and kind mum my sister and I have known her to be if she had.

I knew that if she could find the courage to forgive him, I had to as well; otherwise the bitterness would eat away at me. He hadn't hurt me directly, but I was so angry with him for all that he had put my mum, my uncle and my nan through. Sometimes we can hang on to pain on other people's behalf, holding grudges against those who have wronged the people we love, even when they have forgiven the perpetrator. As far as I know, he never said sorry to the people he hurt, and of course now that he's gone he'll never be able to, but the principle of forgiveness remains the same. Over the years I've forgiven him so many times. It hasn't been a one-off decision, but something I've had to do repeatedly... and I choose to do again today.[5]

Forgiving yourself

Sometimes the hardest person to forgive is yourself.

We've all hurt people. Whether it was a small comment that caused pain or we've perpetrated a bigger crime, none of us has a clean slate. The guilt we can feel is helpful, in that it shows us we've done something wrong. We want to take responsibility for our actions and do what we can to make amends and behave differently in the future. But once we've done what we can to put the situation right, we have to forgive ourselves, because sitting in guilt ultimately becomes self-destructive.

When I do something wrong – let's say I shout at one of my kids – I feel bad. I realise I was tired, it wasn't their fault and they didn't deserve it. So I say sorry, and they say it's fine and carry on with their day, while I ruminate on the situation for hours. I beat myself up for speaking to them like that when I want to show them love and care. I convince myself that I'm a terrible dad and don't deserve them. I end up in a bad place and, honestly, it doesn't even stop me doing it the next time I'm tired, so it serves no purpose in bringing positive change. It's pointless.

We all fall short of our own values from time to time – sometimes in small ways, sometimes in big ones. We need to accept what has happened, seek forgiveness, do what we can to lessen the risks of the same thing happening again, and move on. Shame and guilt are two very different animals. We all make mistakes, but we all have an intrinsic value that's not earned by good behaviour; it's ours because we're human beings. The key is to learn from our mistakes and use them to become kinder people.

Changing perspective

In situations that aren't violent and/or traumatic, taking the perspective of the person who has hurt us can sometimes help us to see the situation differently.

Pressure points

What pressures might the person have been under that could have led to them behaving the way they did?

Past experiences

What background factors might have contributed to the person's behaviour?

Personality type

What might have happened in the person's life to lead them to have the personality traits they have?

Provocations

What behaviours of our own could have provoked the situation? What might the other party have perceived as provocation?

Purpose

What were the other person's intentions? Did they think they were helping in any way?

A better place

'Take a seat please, Mr Regan.'

I'm back at King's College Hospital, where I have spent many days over the last few years waiting to see the consultant who will ask me about my physical and mental health. I usually begin to panic during the long wait, but this time I reflect on how the last ten years of constant hospital appointments and operations have changed me.

To say that I have been on a journey of self-discovery is an understatement. The process of going through surgery, of the pain of months of recovery, of much of normal life being stripped away, has changed me. The surprising thing is that, despite the pain, anxiety, depression, and spiritual and emotional turmoil, I am in a far better place today.

I have let go of the need for black-and-white answers about suffering, and I am becoming more comfortable with the mystery and uncertainty of life. (I now realise that thinking I ever had any control over it was just an illusion.) I am a sensitive soul and, instead of fighting that, I am accepting it is who I am and that's OK. I no longer believe I need to 'toughen up'. I am driven by love and compassion for myself and others, rather than a need to succeed and prove myself.

While I am still passionate about what I do, I no longer want to work every hour of the day. I'm learning to recognise and accept my limitations, and to say no on a regular basis. I acknowledge that my thoughts are not always my friends, and that my illness is not my identity. I am a strong, sensitive and caring person who loves deeply. Having anxious, sad and angry thoughts is something that happens to me, but it doesn't define me.

In short: I am slowly learning to accept myself.

Self-acceptance

Self-acceptance is:

- Being aware of our strengths and weaknesses
- Realistically appraising our talents, capabilities and worth
- The feeling of being content with ourselves, despite our flaws and regardless of past choices

Self-acceptance is not:

- Obsessing over ourselves
- Being arrogant or pretending we have no flaws
- Refusing to admit to weaknesses or to do anything about them
- A belief that we can never change[1]

Self-acceptance is accepting who we are today, regardless of who we want to be tomorrow, and knowing that we have value. It's celebrating our strengths and not feeling a diminished sense of self-worth for our weaknesses. Some say that self-acceptance can help us control our emotions and forgive ourselves for our mistakes, as well as increase our self-confidence, help us be more self-compassionate and allow us to express our true selves.[2]

Understanding the shadow side

The danger in talking about self-acceptance is that we can think it is simply about loving ourselves more. Though self-love is vital for us to flourish, self-acceptance is far more than that – it's also the awareness that we all have a 'shadow side'. We must recognise that and accept both sides of ourselves.

Author Peter Scazzero explains our shadow side by saying, 'Your shadow is the accumulation of untamed emotions, less-than pure motives and thoughts that, while largely unconscious, strongly influence and shape your behaviors. It is the damaged but mostly hidden version of who you are.'[3] This shadow may show up in obvious ways – such as anger, jealousy, resentment and greed – or more subtly in needing to rescue others, overworking, needing to be liked by other people, or rigidity in attitudes and beliefs.

Scazzero talks about how our gifts all have shadow sides to them, and I've seen this fine line between strengths and weaknesses in my own life. For example, I want to do things excellently, which is a good thing, but the flip side is that I can slip into perfectionism. That doesn't serve me well, and can also mean I put unfair expectations on others. Another strength I have is that I am empathetic, but if I'm not careful that can lead to emotional burnout. I'm sure you can apply this technique to your own strengths.

Often, it's challenging circumstances that highlight what's going on. During the Covid pandemic I realised that my love of speaking to groups of people had a shadow side. I had started to rely on the affirmation and encouragement I would usually receive afterwards to make me feel good about myself. Although it was painful to admit this, it was also really helpful to reflect on my motives and redress the balance. It's tempting to try to hide these parts of ourselves – even trying to kid ourselves about what we're doing and why we're doing it – but the more self-accepting we become, the more we will be able to view ourselves in a realistic light, without judgement.

Why do we struggle to accept ourselves?

- We're taught that thinking we're good at something is 'big-headed'.

- There are many industries that thrive on making us think life would be better if we could be a bit *more* something or a bit *less* something else.

- We're not always honest with each other. We think someone else has it all together, and unless they tell us the truth (which is always that they *haven't* got it all together!), we go on believing the lie.

- We blame ourselves if others don't like us, rather than acknowledging that, while we have flaws, we are worthy of love and respect.

- Perfectionism keeps us trapped in believing there is a way to be perfect and that we just need to try harder to get there.

- We believe it when people say unkind things about us. They often tap into our deepest fears about ourselves.

- From an early age we're taught that we're not acceptable as we are, even by those closest to us. They may have had good intentions, but are often acting out of their own fears and wounds.

- We're taught we need to work harder, achieve more, be better... We're rarely told we're enough just as we are.

Not enough

I spent much of my time at school telling myself, *I am not intelligent enough*. As an adult I've had the same fear when I've been asked to debate a topic on a news programme or speak at a conference. I assume I must be there by mistake. When I was working with young people in Peckham, I felt like I wasn't 'urban' enough and doubted whether the kids would relate to me. All my life in church I have felt like I'm not spiritual enough. I have so many questions and don't seem to have the clear black-and-white views some of my friends do. Sometimes it feels like I don't have enough faith.

Not intelligent enough, not urban enough, not spiritual enough... not enough, not enough, not enough. That thought has played on a loop for as long as I can remember, even though no one has ever said those words to me. Where do these thoughts start? As kids our brains are like sponges. We take note of people's facial expressions, the volume of their voices, the way they interact with others and the way they treat us. We all want to be loved and accepted, so we try to please people and find out what is acceptable to them so that we can be loved. If we see we have behaved in an unacceptable way to the people caring for us, we often seek to hide that part of ourselves, determining that it isn't loveable or acceptable. As kids we often can't distinguish between ourselves and our behaviour – we think if we do something wrong, there is something wrong with us.

Once I started to recognise that it was my inner critic who was constantly telling me I wasn't enough, I tried telling him to be quiet. He wouldn't listen. So I tried a different technique: I tried to recognise when I was being harsh on myself, and then pause and consider what I could replace the negative thought with. Sometimes I used a journal to get the thoughts out of my head and recognise them for what they were. These things have helped me realise that even with my flaws I am wanted, loved, unique and valued.

What's the point?

Our inner critic is there for a reason. That's not to say we should listen to it and let it run the show, but we should take a look at what's driving it.

When people are asked to picture their inner critic, we get some interesting results. Sometimes we realise it's the voice of someone who has done us some harm in life – perhaps an angry parent, a teacher who hurt us, an old boss who bullied us, a person at school who enjoyed belittling us. Sometimes there is a cultural source, a voice telling us this is how the perfect man or woman should behave, or how we should be acting based on our cultural heritage.

Take a minute to picture yours. Who is that person? What do they look like, sound like, dress like? What are their motives when they criticise you? Are they (misguidedly) trying to protect you from harm? How could you respond with compassion to your inner critic while also acknowledging that they are holding you back rather than serving you well?

Types of inner critic

Psychotherapist Jay Earley and Internal Family Systems clinician Bonnie Weiss identified seven different types of inner critic, each with its own motivation.

Perfectionist

This critic wants you to fit in and not be rejected, so it pushes you to do everything to the highest standard.

Inner controller

The fear of this critic is that you will indulge too much (food, drink, sex, etc.), so it shames you to try to protect you from yourself.

Taskmaster

Being lazy is the worst thing this critic can imagine, so it insists you must work hard and be successful.

Underminer

Don't take risks! That's the key for this inner critic. If you don't take risks, you won't get hurt or rejected, so it tries to undermine your self-confidence to keep you 'safe'.

Destroyer

If there has been deprivation and/or trauma in your early years, this critic can come into play, undermining your self-worth and shaming you into believing you are flawed, and don't deserve basic care and respect.

Guilt-tripper

To avoid you repeating mistakes from your past, this critic keeps replaying them and won't let you move on. It fears that if you forget or find freedom, the same thing will happen again.

Conformist

The goal here is for you to be liked and admired by others. The tactic? To fit in at all costs.[4]

Self-compassion

Cultivating self-acceptance means cultivating self-compassion. Compassion means to suffer with, to be conscious of another's distress and to have a desire to alleviate that pain... so self-compassion means to be able to do that for yourself.

Self-compassion is not:

- Self-indulgence. The voice telling us to have an extra glass of wine to take the edge off, to eat more cake, to get lost in another episode of a Netflix series.
- Self-esteem. The way we feel about ourselves.
- Self-pity. Where we make everything into a drama that's all about us.
- The easy way out. It's giving ourselves the kindness we need and deserve, not telling ourselves that we don't have to change.

One of the quickest exercises we can do to help ourselves be more self-compassionate is to treat ourselves as we would treat a friend.

Think about a situation where you've been highly critical of yourself. It might be a one-off mistake or something you do continually that you find frustrating about yourself (e.g., I comfort eat when I'm sad, I get angry really quickly). Imagine your closest friend is struggling with that same thing. What would you say to them? Now say it to yourself. You deserve that same love and compassion.

But I'm not

Rachel told me that when she was in her twenties, she spent a lot of time in a group of friends where she always felt like the odd one out. She was quiet, whereas the other girls in the group seemed to be much more confident. They were happy to be centre stage, whereas she shied away from it. They liked to make people laugh and always provided lots of entertainment. Rachel would go home after a night together and think, *I should be more like them. I wish I was louder, funnier, more exciting.*

Years later, she spoke to one of those friends about it and was surprised by her response. 'Are you kidding?!' Lorna said. 'I always wanted to be more like you! I always came away from those evenings thinking I was such an idiot. Why couldn't I just shut up rather than always making a fool of myself? I always admired that you were so kind and thoughtful with people. I wished I could be more like you.'

Rachel said it was a real turning point in her journey to self-acceptance.

She had different strengths and weaknesses from her friends, but it didn't make her any better or worse. In some of the qualities she found hard to accept in herself, others could see things to admire. Some of the qualities she admired in others, they found uncomfortable in themselves. It made her realise that there are good and bad things about all personality traits, and she needed to accept herself for who she was, rather than comparing herself unfavourably to others.

Heartbreakingly beautiful

Jean has been an ambassador for Kintsugi Hope from the start, and a short time ago was diagnosed with terminal cancer. Reflecting on her diagnosis and the days to follow, she shared:

> It's scary when you've been told there's nothing they can do and you've only got six months left to live! It has all happened so quickly. Looking for things to be thankful for isn't easy, but do you know, I think I may have found it!
>
> I've never felt truly loved. My parents were very busy and had problems of their own, so I never felt good enough. I was always being compared to my very clever twin brother. I have worked hard to be open, honest and vulnerable, and in doing so my relationships have improved – especially the one with myself. Since my diagnosis I have been showered with flowers and beautiful messages, and I have never felt so loved. So while I'm sure God didn't have a part in my diagnosis, I am beginning to believe that he has turned it around to complete my story... Jean is lovable![5]

My favourite author, Henri Nouwen, writes, 'I have come to realize that the greatest trap in our life is not success, popularity, and power, but self-rejection. ... Self-rejection is the greatest enemy of the spiritual life because it contradicts the sacred voice that calls us the "Beloved".'[6]

Let's not wait till we're near the end of our lives to know that we're loved. The truth is, the people who are close to you are under no illusions that you're perfect. They see your flaws, they know that you have good days and bad days, and they love you regardless. It can be tempting to keep people at arm's length, to try to only show the good sides of ourselves, but that doesn't give them an opportunity to truly love us. Each and every one of us is a combination of things, good and bad. If we let people in and show them who we really are, if we listen when they tell us they love us, we will know that we are truly loved.

When you feel like shit

My inner critic was laying into me. I was about to give a talk at a church service in America that had some special guests: around 200 members of the homeless community. I'd visited the shelter they were staying at the day before, and spent some time with them and the shelter's manager. The residents were struggling with high levels of anxiety, depression and other mental illnesses. Many had physical health conditions as a result of living on the streets. Some felt spiritually lost, as it seemed that even the God they believed in had abandoned them. Many were understandably angry at how unfair it was that they were living in such difficult circumstances. The manager said that for all the varied problems they were facing, the biggest was that the guys staying there 'felt like shit'. 'Their self-esteem is broken, smashed to pieces,' he added. 'My job is to do everything I can to nurture hope.'

As I prepared to speak that morning, I couldn't get what he'd said out of my head. What could I possibly say that might help? What hope could I offer? Then I remembered an illustration I had used when speaking to people in Trenchtown, Jamaica, who had been facing similar struggles with their self-worth.

I stood at the front of the church and took out a $5 bill. 'Who wants it?' I asked. Hands went up all over the room. I screwed it up and said, 'Anyone still want it?' They nodded. Then I threw it on the floor, trampling it underfoot until it was dirty. 'Who wants it now?' The hands continued to wave, though people's faces were puzzled, wondering what on earth I was doing.

'Why do you want it?' I asked. 'Is it because, despite the fact it's been screwed up and downtrodden, it's still worth exactly the same as it was at the start?

'I don't understand why life is so cruel at times,' I continued. 'I have no answers, but I do believe that whatever we have been through, however others have made us feel, whatever choices we've made that we've regretted, however we've been treated, we all still have worth. No matter what, we are still valuable. When we live as if we believe we have worth and accept ourselves, change often follows.'

I quickly sat down and looked at the floor, unsure how my words would land. Within seconds I heard clapping, and was moved to tears seeing people spring up from their seats to give me a standing ovation – something I had never experienced before (or since).

I am deeply aware that people need practical support as well as words, but I've also seen how quickly self-belief vanishes when life is hard. We all need to know that we bring value to the world just by being us. Something beautiful happens to us internally when we start to believe it. All of us struggle with our worth at times. It doesn't matter where we live, what job we do or what our social status is – none of us is immune. But next time you're struggling, look at a £5 note and remember that your value doesn't change with your circumstances.

10

Healthy relationships

'If you want to go fast, go alone. If you want to go far, go together.'

African proverb

Created for connection

The need for connection is wired into our DNA. We have many relationships throughout our lives, and they form and shape us, hurt and heal us, frustrate and inspire us. Human connection is so central to us that even when we're born we need physical touch for our survival. Not just someone to feed and clothe us; we need affection. Babies who aren't held can stop growing and, if the lack of physical touch continues, they can even die.[1]

Mother Teresa, who is famous for showing love and care to those in some of the most desperate conditions in India, is often quoted as saying, 'In the West there is a loneliness, which I call the leprosy of the West. In many ways, it is worse than our poor in Calcutta.'[2]

While we have even more ways to stay in touch with one another than when Mother Teresa was alive, we continue to be a society plagued by loneliness, with one in four adults reporting feeling lonely some or all of the time.[3] Loneliness isn't just an excruciating feeling; it can damage our physical health too. A 2020 study on social isolation and loneliness in older adults found that, among other damaging effects, loneliness is associated with the following:

- An increased risk of premature death from all causes, to rival that of deaths caused by smoking, obesity and physical inactivity.
- A 50 per cent increased risk of dementia.
- A 29 per cent increased risk of heart disease and a 32 per cent increased risk of stroke.
- Higher rates of depression, anxiety and suicide.
- Among heart failure patients, a nearly four times increased risk of death, 68 per cent increased risk of hospitalisation, and 57 per cent increased risk of emergency department visits.[4]

There is no doubt about it: we need to find ways to develop and nurture relationships where we feel connected, known and loved. For some of us that means being courageous enough to let down our guard and allow others to see the real us. For some it will mean evaluating the health of our current relationships, considering redrawing healthy boundaries and perhaps even stepping away from relationships that have become toxic.

Healthy and unhealthy behaviours in friendships

Green flags

They make time for you.

They listen and express empathy.

They celebrate your successes.

They show kindness in small ways (texts on the day of an important work meeting, a card on your birthday, an offer of help when you're in need).

They want the best for you.

They encourage you and see your strengths.

They are honest with you about themselves and the highs and lows of their lives.

They accept that you aren't perfect and love you regardless.

Red flags

They are jealous of your successes.

They put you down and make harsh remarks (even if they're disguised as jokes).

They try to tell you what to do.

They ignore your boundaries.

They are disengaged – they don't respond to messages or initiate contact.

They like to bring up your mistakes and focus on your weaknesses.

They like to make out everything is always perfect in their life.

They have a lack of empathy.

They leave you feeling like you're not good enough.

They try to discourage you from having other relationships, even with existing family and friends.

They talk at you rather than with you.

They share your secrets.

Where does it all begin?

The relationships we have with our parents or caregivers when we're babies have a huge impact on the ways we continue to form and respond to relationships as adults. We're all born with a desire for comfort and consistency from those around us, and we have no control over whether we get that or not. Every parent is only human, and there are many reasons they might not be physically or emotionally present in a child's life. (I'm not here to knock parents. As a dad of four, I know we need all the grace that can be extended to us.) Most of us do what our own parents did, which can have positive and negative effects. Often we can see patterns of behaviour ripple down through the generations. But that doesn't mean they can't be changed. Our minds are malleable and able to form new thinking patterns. New relationships and being connected to a wider community can make a huge difference.

For all of us, understanding ourselves and our attachment styles can only be a helpful thing. It's not about finding new labels to stick to ourselves or excuses to behave in certain ways. It's about knowing why we might be the way we are, which empowers us to choose something different.

Anxious attachment

If we have an anxious attachment style, we are likely to need constant reassurance that we are loved and needed, and will do anything to avoid rejection and criticism. This can result in people-pleasing behaviour and a desire to avoid conflict at all costs. The idea of people's disapproval can eat away at us, constantly playing on our minds as we worry what other people think.

Avoidant attachment

When intimacy feels scary, this can indicate an avoidant attachment style. This often happens when parents have been emotionally unavailable, and when a child has tried to connect with a parent and failed. It leads to us trying to steer clear of deep connection with others and find ways of coping alone. Talking about feelings does not come naturally. That's not to say those of us with this attachment style don't want relationships at all; it may just be harder to let our guard down and trust people. We have to find people we feel safe being vulnerable with, which often takes a long time.

Disorganised attachment

If our parents have been very unreliable and inconsistent, and had difficulties dealing with tough emotions in response to stress, we can develop a disorganised attachment. This is categorised by an extreme fear of abandonment, and chaotic and unpredictable relationship patterns. As children we may have been forced to rely on a parent we found frightening, and as a result we may struggle to feel safe in relationships. This attachment style may be displayed in wanting intimacy one minute and then pushing someone away the next.

Secure attachment

This is formed when a child feels safe to express their needs and is able to go into the world able to show distress when they are unhappy. Research found that infants who were securely attached to their mothers showed less anxiety and a more positivity mindset towards the relationship, probably because they felt assured that their mother would respond to their needs.[5]

If you recognise yourself in the anxious, avoidant or disorganised attachment styles, this doesn't mean you can't change the way you respond in relationships. These are all learned behaviours, so the good news is that we can unlearn them too. Knowing more about attachment styles can help us understand ourselves and others we are in relationship with.

Understanding empathy

I used to think that empathy was feeling the same feelings as someone else, but I now realise that's not actually possible. We are all different: we have different pasts, different presents, different bodies, different outlooks on the world, different expectations, and different emotional styles and skills. No one can walk in someone else's shoes, so we do them a disservice when we say that we 100 per cent know how they feel.

Sometimes we think it's obvious what someone is feeling. Say their dad has just been diagnosed with cancer and we assume they are devastated. Many would be, but for some people things are more complicated – perhaps things have been historically difficult, and they feel more detached. Jumping in with assumptions can make people feel alienated – as though their response is wrong.

Psychologist Carl Rogers, who founded the person-centred approach to psychotherapy, reportedly said that empathy is 'the listener's effort to hear the other person deeply, accurately, and nonjudgmentally'.[6] I love that. It's a much more helpful way of understanding empathy. Empathy is key to successful relationships, and you can't rush it. You have to take the time to listen to what someone is saying and feeling. It's not about us or how we would react in their situation. It's not about jumping in with solutions or moving the conversation on when we feel uncomfortable. It's about focusing on the speaker. Next time someone is struggling, try saying something like this:

That sounds really difficult.
No wonder you're upset.
Would you like to tell me more about that?
Would you like some advice or for me to be a listening ear?
I'm here for you.
I can see why you found that situation painful.

I think what you're saying is... Have I understood what you meant?
I'm so sorry you're having to deal with this.
I really admire the way you're handling this.
Whatever you decide, I'll support you.

I can't fix this

When people ask me what one of the hardest lessons I have had to learn in relationships is, it is this: I can't fix people or situations, as much as I may want to. My ego will try to tell me that I have all the solutions and that I know what's best for people, but I should know better than to listen to my ego.

I had a friend who I suspected was in a violent relationship, though she had never said anything. There were signs of dominance, control, insecurity and pain. One night when I dropped her home she started chatting about her partner and I asked, 'Does he ever get angry?' 'Oh yeah,' she said matter of factly. 'Does he ever hit you?' I asked. When she nodded, I rushed in, 'Leave him! You can stay with me and Diane – come home with me now!' She shrugged it off and said it had only happened a couple of times.

She told me to let it go, so I dropped her home and spent a sleepless night wondering if I'd done the right thing. Part of me wanted to storm in and drag her to safety. The other part of me knew that was a huge overstep and it wasn't my decision to make. She didn't need my judgement or for me to rescue her; she needed a friend she could talk to – someone who would be there for her whether she stayed in that relationship or not.

Thankfully, she did choose to get to a place of safety, and Diane and I were able to support her, but it made me think about how often I rush in. I want to be a safe person, someone who can be trusted and who listens – about the big and the small stuff. I want my friends to know they can be themselves around me – bringing their strengths and weaknesses, their vulnerabilities and their victories. It made me think about what it means to hold space for someone; a place where they can be real and honest. I came across this definition by author Heather Plett:

It means that we are willing to walk alongside another person in whatever journey they're on without judging them, making them feel inadequate, trying to fix them, or trying to impact the outcome. When we hold space for other people, we open our hearts, offer unconditional support, and let go of judgement and control.[7]

I love that. To put it into practice, I need to leave my ego out of it. I am not the rescuer. My friends and family are capable of making their own decisions, and I need to let them. I am not here to control or manipulate them, and I'm not in relationship with them to pursue my own agenda. The healthiest relationships are the ones built on mutual trust, empathy, communication and compromise. No power imbalance, no hidden agenda; just love.

Boundaries

For many years, my belief was that to be a good friend I needed to be constantly available to people; to be there for them whatever they needed and whenever they needed it. I would run myself ragged trying to be all things to all people, then beat myself up for failing to achieve this ridiculous standard. I genuinely thought I was a bad friend. I heard people talk about boundaries and thought people who enforced those must be really lacking in compassion. It took me a long time to realise that boundaries actually help improve relationships and enable us to love more authentically.

If we have healthy boundaries where we are caring for our own wellbeing, we are more likely to have the energy and emotional capacity to care for others. It's easy to overcommit to helping people and then resent the fact that we are exhausted and depleted when it wasn't their fault for asking; it was ours for saying yes when we should have said no.

If you're trying to work out if you have good boundaries, ask yourself these questions:

- Do you find it difficult to say no to people?
- Do you constantly feel guilty that you aren't able to do more or be more?
- Are you continually exhausted and rushed off your feet?
- Do you regularly over-promise and then panic when you can't under-deliver?
- Are you known as someone who will do anything for anyone – at any cost?

I have a tendency to be a people-pleaser; I want to make everyone happy, and that can be at the expense of what makes me happy. I feel uncomfortable when I say no, worrying that I've offended or let someone down. The belief underpinning this is that my needs are less important than anyone else's. Swallowing our own needs doesn't help anyone and can lead to us becoming bitter. We have to know what we need and what our boundaries are, so we can love people from that place. We sometimes wish that our friends, partners, parents and colleagues knew what we needed without us having to say, but it's unfair and unrealistic to expect people to be mind-readers.

Boundaries are also key in setting expectations for healthy relationships. They are not about controlling other people – they don't involve telling someone else what to do – but they are about being clear in terms of what you need. True friends will respect your boundaries and be pleased you are looking after yourself. The people who will be angry? Those who benefit from you *not* having boundaries. They will likely push against them, perhaps try to make you feel guilty or continue with behaviour that you've said is unacceptable. You telling someone what your boundaries are doesn't mean they will respect them – after all, they're your boundaries, not theirs. To hold firm to your boundaries you have to know their importance, and believe that you are worthy of having your own needs met and of being treated in a loving and respectful manner. As Brené Brown says, 'Daring to set boundaries is about having the courage to love ourselves, even when we risk disappointing others.'[8]

Relationships can change from being healthy to toxic when people stop respecting each other's boundaries; likewise, a difficult relationship can be restored when healthy boundaries are set in place.

When to walk away

Some friendships are for a season and, like many romantic relationships, even the deepest friendships – the ones you thought would be for life – can break down. Good relationships are worth fighting for, but not all relationships are, and it can be incredibly painful to walk away. Here are some of the signs that it may be time to let go:

- They shut you down when you try to talk about something real.
- You're always the one who calls, messages or suggests catching up.
- You leave interactions with the person feeling worse than you did before.
- You are sticking with it out of obligation.
- You are compromising your integrity and boundaries to try to keep the peace.
- You have nothing in common except your past.
- There's more competition between you than support and respect.
- You consistently feel like you give more than you get back.
- You're the only one fighting for the relationship to continue.

Therapist Nedra Glover Tawwab says, 'It can be healthy to slowly move away from friendships that no longer speak to who you are and to do so without drama. You don't need to let people go completely, but you can spend less time in situations that no longer add value.'9 This is a really helpful reminder that we don't always need to make big declarations, pick a fight or tell someone they are no longer welcome in our life. Sometimes we can simply choose to spend less time with them. For the times we do need to address the fact we're ending a relationship, Tawwab suggests some helpful phrases:

- For my wellbeing, I need to end this relationship.
- This is really hard for me to say: I don't want to be in this relationship any more.
- I've tried to make this work and I don't want to fight any more to keep this together.
- This relationship isn't working for me. I need to end it.

Walking away is rarely easy, but sometimes it's the most important thing we can do for our mental and emotional wellbeing.

Where are you at?

Think about the different relationships in your life – some examples are listed below. For each one, rate how content you are with the state of play right now on a scale of 1–10.

Parents
Siblings
Partner
Children
Friends you speak to regularly
Friends you speak to less often
Colleagues
In-laws
Other

If there were one or two you could improve, which would they be?

What action could you take this week that would nudge things in the right direction?

What are the three most important things to you in a relationship? Ask someone who is close to you the same question, and see where you differ and where you overlap.

'Holding space' by Jane Smith

Holding space for someone
Is so important,
Being genuine,
Kind and supportive,
Not interrupting
To tell your own story
Or changing the subject
To bring yourself glory.
Not trying to 'fix' everything
By offering solutions
But being attentive
And willing to listen.
Not being in a hurry
To offer advice
But comfortable with
Moments of quiet.

Holding space for someone
Is to journey with them
Without judgement
Or criticism.
Not making assumptions
Or speaking platitudes
But striving to have
A tolerant attitude.
Not 'silver lining' everything
With false positivity,
Nor providing answers
To all of life's difficulties,
But coming alongside
To gently encourage,
Build resilience
And help them to manage.[10]

11

Resilience

Resilience is not the ability to bounce back; it's the ability to bounce forwards.

Not bouncing back

Have you ever gone through something really difficult and been offered the cheerful refrain, 'Don't worry, you'll bounce back'? People often think resilience means bouncing back, as though we're elastic bands than can be stretched and then return to our previous shape.

Chris Johnstone, in his book *Seven Ways to Build Resilience*, talks about the difference between a tennis ball and a tomato. If you squeeze a tennis ball, it pops back immediately. If you throw it against the ground, it bounces back. In contrast, do the same to a tomato and all you get is a mess. Johnstone points out that this is only one view of resilience. What happens if you bury a tomato and a tennis ball in soil? After a number of years, the ball will likely have started to decompose and be useless. On the other hand, given the right circumstances, the seeds in the tomato may have taken root and given birth to new life. You could find new vines ripe with fresh, juicy tomatoes. Johnstone says, 'When adversity is followed by new growth, where we rise again but in a different form, we can think of this as "bouncing forward".'[1]

We can't wipe the pain from our lives, so we have a choice: try to ignore it and allow it to break us; or work with it and see if it can lead us somewhere new.

The hard things I have been through have challenged my values. They have forced me to ask, 'What are the most important things to me? What are my priorities?' Adversity has sometimes made me face up to things I was hoping never to have to confront. I hope that what I've been through has also made me less judgemental, and a softer, kinder person to others and myself.

Resilience is not...

- Pushing through and battling on, even when it's breaking you
- Having a stiff upper lip and telling yourself to 'get over it'
- Being immune to life's challenges and pain
- Repressing our emotions and putting on a mask
- Having no needs or weaknesses
- Permanent/toxic positivity
- Putting up with things you shouldn't
- Always saying yes
- Always being able to get up after you have been knocked down
- Being inexhaustible
- Having no boundaries
- Putting yourself last
- Trying harder
- Being strong for someone else at the expense of being authentic
- Neglecting your own needs

When muscles break

When body builders want to increase their muscle capacity, they know the muscles need to tear. They push themselves further by gradually increasing the weights they lift. It hurts, but this intentional pain increases their ability, because the breakage in the muscle fibres causes the body to repair the muscle, which is what makes it stronger. In a similar way, going through difficult and challenging times in our lives – things that feel stretching, and at times as though they've broken us – can have the ability to strengthen us.

An important lesson from our body-building friends, though: rest plays a huge part in the growth. They don't keep going, adding more weight each time without pausing. This could cause irreparable damage. Instead, they know to rest. During that time of rest, the body does its essential work and brings the healing the muscle needs. We need to recognise when we emotionally need to stop and rest, allowing ourselves to repair and strengthen in order to continue. Taking time out can be difficult, but it is vital.

One last tip: the other thing a muscle needs in order to grow is the right nutrition. For resilience, we need to find ways to consistently feed our mind, spirit and soul in healthy ways.

The resilience river

One of the most helpful analogies for me on resilience was given in a talk by holistic medicine pioneer and local GP, Professor Patrick Pietroni. Summarising Pietroni's words in *Seven Ways to Build Resilience*, Johnstone writes:

> Being well and healthy... is a bit like rowing a boat. Illness, or other kinds of problems, can be thought of as crashing into a rock... Most approaches to tackling difficulties tend to focus on the rock... But the problem, or rock, is only half the story. The water level... represents our background level of resilience. When we're feeling good in ourselves, with our emotional reserves at a high level, we may float over the rocks that on a bad day we'd hit. When we're feeling depleted, our water levels low, we're more likely to crash.[2]

What keeps your water level high? What brings it lower? There will probably be some common ground for most of us. A lack of sleep, a stressful situation at work or home, a bad diet and being too busy can lower the water level, while rest, relaxation and healthy relationships can help bring it back up. There are, of course, other things that are more personal to us as individuals that bring us life. I found it really helpful to write some of these things down to get some concrete ideas on what helps me and what hinders me. What brings my resilience levels low is being tired, working too hard, holding on to relationships that aren't working and listening to my inner critic. Some of the things that raise my water levels are self-compassion, exercise, prayer and safe relationships. How about you?

Things that raise your resilience:

-
-
-
-
-

Things that lower your resilience:

-
-
-
-
-

Acceptance is key

When our circumstances are hard, it's natural to want to fight against them. That makes sense when those circumstances are within our control, because taking action can bring about positive change. But what about the things we can't change? Imagine you find yourself in the middle of some quicksand (something films in the 1980s led us to believe was a distinct possibility). Your likely immediate reaction is to try your hardest to get out, but the problem with quicksand is that the more you struggle, the more you sink. Crazy as it seems, the way to get free is to stop struggling and lie as calmly and as flat as you can. This spreads your body weight out and allows you to roll yourself to safety.

Admiral James Stockdale was in a prisoner of war camp in Vietnam in the 1960s, where he faced torture and didn't know if he would ever be released or see his loved ones again. Despite the horrific circumstances, he was convinced that, no matter what happened, he could turn this experience into a defining moment in his life that he wouldn't want to trade for anything else.

Eventually, he made it out, and when asked years later, 'Who didn't make it out?', he quickly replied that it was the optimists, the ones who said, 'We're going to be out by Christmas.' Christmas would come and go, and they'd say, 'We're going to be out by Easter.' But that too would come and go with no change.[3] It sounds like they had the right attitude: think positively, keep your hopes up and everything will be OK. This is often the pseudo-spiritual advice perpetuated by our society, when in actual fact, this wishful thinking did them no good. Instead, it crushed their spirits and broke their hearts.

Jim Collins, author of *Good to Great*, calls the attitude of Admiral Stockdale the 'Stockdale Paradox'. He describes this as the ability to maintain an unflinching belief that you can succeed, teamed with the commitment to facing the current realities of life, however difficult they may be.[4]

Facing up to the facts isn't giving up or failing; it's about acknowledging the reality of your circumstances and accepting them, saying that even if there will come a day when things are different, this is the life you are living today.

Finding meaning

When I was feeling very broken, someone said to me, 'Patrick, shit happens. Get over it and stop trying to find meaning in it.' I've never been a fan of the saying, 'Everything happens for a reason', but surely trying to find some meaning can't be a bad thing? I had no choice about the season I was in, but I really hoped some good could come out of it.

When Diane and I started Kintsugi Hope we wanted to help others facing similar struggles, but not in our wildest dreams did we expect it to grow to the level it has. Thousands of people have joined groups across the country, facilitated by their peers. Courses take place in coffee shops, pubs, schools, universities, prisons, hairdressers, community groceries, police stations and homeless shelters.

The feedback from head teachers, doctors and others taking part has been amazing. There are so many stories of people gaining confidence and realising they are not alone. Those who were feeling overwhelmed by life have found the tools to flourish, and some even said that the course saved their lives. I'm not pretending it's all been smooth-sailing and there haven't been some tough days, but I am so grateful for what has happened and that our pain was able to act as a catalyst for something so positive.

In the well-known book *Man's Search for Meaning*, Austrian psychiatrist and Auschwitz survivor Viktor E. Frankl describes a turning point for him in the camp. He was on his way to work for a particularly sadistic man and was disgusted at how meaningless his life felt. He knew he needed a sense of purpose if he was to survive, so he imagined giving lectures on the psychology of the concentration camp to help outsiders understand what he had been through. He had no way of knowing if he would survive to give those lectures, but having a goal helped. He said, 'We must never forget that we may also find meaning in life even when confronted with a hopeless situation, when facing a fate that cannot be changed.'[5]

Adapting

One characteristic of resilient people is their ability to adapt and make the most of whatever they have at hand, instead of complaining and focusing on what they don't have. In concentration camps, resilient inmates knew to pocket pieces of string or wire whenever they found them. The string or wire might later become useful – to fix a pair of shoes, perhaps, which in freezing conditions might make the difference between life and death. This process of using what is at hand to create something new is called bricolage. We saw this many times during the Covid-19 pandemic, whether it was people using creative means to keep their businesses afloat or to help their kids learn from home. When situations unravel, bricoleurs muddle through, imagining possibilities where others are confounded.

How could you use the resources currently at your disposal to make something new?

'Without the rain' by Jane Smith

Without the rain
There would be no rainbow.
Without the pain
There would be no birth.
Without the future
There would be no tomorrow.
Without the treasure
There would be no worth.
Without the illness
There would be no recovery.
Without the sickness
There would be no health.
Without the difficulty
There would be no opportunity.
Without the poverty
There would be no wealth.
Without the learning
There would be no wisdom.
Without the mercy
There would be no grace.
Without the hindsight
There would be no understanding.
Without the insight
There would be no gain.
Without the music
There would be no harmony.
Without the voices
There would be no choir.
Without the waves
There would be no ocean.
Without the flames

Resilience

There would be no fire.
Without the damage
There would be no mending.
Without the challenge
There would be no growth.
Without the courage
There would be no progress.
Without the message
There would be no hope.[6]

No happily ever after

Growing up, one of my favourite people in the world was my Uncle Barry. He'd had a really difficult life. His dad left when he was young, after a violent relationship with his mum, and they had very little money. He was in and out of work, and lost his brother in middle age. After his marriage broke down, he had a string of other broken relationships. Despite all of this, he was kind and generous, and I always felt safe around him as he was so non-judgemental. When I was a child, we spent every Saturday together watching football, and he was one of my best friends.

Barry suffered very badly with mental ill health, and it would not be uncommon for me to get a call to say that he had been sectioned again. Barry had lots of support offered to him, yet the trauma of the past was too much and he often rejected help, leaving the rest of the family frustrated.

A few years ago, Barry had a fall and was virtually paralysed, leaving him bedridden. He was sent to specialist hospitals to try to help him regain movement, but he wouldn't do the exercises they set him, as he said they were too painful. He ended up in a care home, and although they tried to help him, he was noncompliant most of the time. He spent his days lying in bed watching TV, with occasional visitors standing outside his window to say hello (this happened during Covid).

I wish I could tell you this was a story with a happy ending, but it's not. My Uncle Barry died earlier this year. So why share it with you? It reminds me of two things: one, people are loveable no matter what. Yes, we wanted Barry to find more freedom and healing, to do his exercises and get out of bed, but that didn't mean we didn't love him regardless. Two: it reminds me to take the help that is being offered in tough times, or to go even further and actually *ask* for the help I need. The truth is that people want to help us – medical professionals, family and friends. Sometimes we just have to let go of whatever is stopping us and say yes.

One time after I'd seen Barry in the care home, I headed off to interview Eva Schloss, Anne Frank's stepsister and Auschwitz survivor. I found myself comparing her with Barry, wondering what had given Eva the strength to make it through this dark time in history. 'How did you keep going?' I asked. Eva replied, 'I was not ready to die. I had goals; I wanted to get married, have a family. I also had a really good mother and father, and a brother who I adored. I would never give up hope a miracle could happen and I would survive.'

She went on to explain that it was harder for her when she was released and was living with survivor's guilt, having lost her dad and brother at the hands of the Nazis. In 1946, she was at the end of herself and wanted to die by suicide. This wasn't a period of time when counselling was freely available. Otto Frank (Anne Frank's dad), who had lost absolutely everything, encouraged her to let go of the hate in her heart and find something to hold on to, just as he had when he found Anne's diary. Eva found her brother's paintings under the floorboards in their house and donated them to the resistance museum so that people could see them. She also wrote a book about his life, and many years later began working on an animated film about him. This gave her a sense of purpose and renewed her spirit. It took her forty years after being released from Auschwitz to be ready to tell her own story, and she now says she encourages people to speak up and share what they find difficult, regardless of what's happened to them.

We will never know why one life turns out so differently from another; why Eva was able to not only survive but to thrive after her trauma, and why Barry couldn't find a way to keep going. He never found any purpose in his pain; never found the hope that would revive his spirit. I believe he tried in his own way, but he didn't have it in him. I don't judge Barry, as I can't say how I would have reacted had I faced the same challenges with the same resources. Not every story has a happy-ever-after, but there's still value to be found in it. When Barry passed away at the age of sixty-three, after catching an infection, I reflected on his legacy. In my formative years he instilled in me the values of being kind, being a safe space for others and being non-judgemental; values that are still important to me today. He left me and our whole family with happy memories, and although his name won't be remembered in the history books, he will always be a big part of my history. I wouldn't be doing the things I am doing today if it weren't for him, and for that I'm very grateful.

What's the story?

We can get stuck with certain narratives in life – the ones others have told us about who we are and what's happened to us, and the ones we tell ourselves. Reframing those stories can bring a huge shift to our thinking, strengthening our resilience in difficult times.

Try writing a new version of a story that causes you pain and worry in your life. For example, if you've seen yourself as the victim of other people's mistakes, you could write about how you've been hurt by others but haven't let that define who you are. If you feel like you've failed to achieve your goals, focus on times when you've put yourself out there and tried, or how you've persevered despite setbacks. Write about the positive values you've displayed, and where you've been the kind of person you wish to be.

Continuing the journey

Where were you at when you first opened this book?

Where are you at now?

It's OK if you find yourself in exactly the same place. In fact, things sometimes have to get worse before they can get better again. We have to acknowledge the brokenness before we can rebuild. Regardless of where you are on your journey right now, I fully believe in the importance of pausing, taking stock, reviewing and celebrating. In fact, that's how our twelve-week Kintsugi Hope Wellbeing courses always end: Review and Celebrate. And so, it felt right to close this book in the same way, holding plenty of space for both.

Review

Here are some questions you may want to consider as you pause and reflect.

As you look back on all you've read in *Brighter Days*, what stands out the most to you?

_____

_____

_____

_____

What have you learned about yourself?

_____

_____

_____

_____

Which attitudes or beliefs about yourself have changed?

_____

_____

_____

_____

With whom would you like to continue to journey these topics?

_____

_____

_____

_____

What would you like to do differently from now on?

_____

_____

_____

_____

How can you make that happen?

_____

_____

_____

_____

Celebrate

The final question we ask each of our Kintsugi Wellbeing Groups is: how will you celebrate the changes in your life? I know that for some of you, your answer to this question might be: *What changes? How am I supposed to celebrate when things still feel so hopeless?* Well, I want to remind you that, regardless of whether you believe it now or not, *brighter days are possible.*

I used to think that having poor mental health was a life sentence, something I had to just put up with. I was tempted to hide it from others and think it was something I needed to deal with on my own. I've learned that change is possible, and that everything feels better when I'm honest with trustworthy people about how I'm feeling.

My biggest prayer for you as you finish turning these pages is that you will hold on to that hope. It has been said that you can only see the stars in the dark, so I hope that no matter how dark things feel, you will see those lights shining – however small and far away they may seem.

I hope *Brighter Days* has made you feel less alone and reminded you that you deserve to be seen, heard and valued. What you do, what you say and who you are matters; your story is sacred. I hope you close this book with the determination to be intentional about investing in your mental health. There is no one quick fix, but there is a myriad of things that will enhance our mental, emotional, behavioural, physical and spiritual wellbeing. While there are loads of ideas in this book, you'll probably have realised there are some common themes: seeking professional help, talking to those we love, being aware of – and challenging – some of the thought patterns we get into, knowing our own value, seeking the gold in the dirt to remind us that life is rarely all one thing, and letting go of old attitudes and grudges that no longer serve us.

So, go back and reread the sections that had the biggest impact on you, underlining anything that stands out. Leave this book somewhere you'll pick it up again and again to dip in and out of, to remind you to keep looking after yourself. Suggest a friend reads it, and that you talk about it together, encouraging one another to try some of the exercises and put into practice the things that will help you. (Remember, the goal isn't that you do *all* of these things, but that you find the things that work for you!) Find a local Kintsugi Wellbeing Group or another local support group to help you continue to explore these themes. Dig out a picture of yourself at a young age and set it as the screen saver on your phone, then use it as a reminder to ask what that person needs and deserves today. Volunteer for a local charity, because kindness is the best drug of all. Pick up a pen and journal to get some thoughts out of your head. Text a friend to meet for a coffee. Say a prayer or go for a walk in the forest, and enjoy feeling enveloped by something bigger than you.

Remember, you are not alone.

There is always hope.

Brighter days are ahead.

Patrick's new company, Brighter Days, is now offering a range of programmes and resources to support people in improving their mental wellbeing. Check out www.brighterdays.life to find out more.

Notes

Introduction

1 'Who are we', Kintsugi Hope: https://kintsugihope.com (accessed 16 June 2023).
2 'Spirituality and Mental Health', Royal College of Psychiatrists: https://www.rcpsych.ac.uk/mental-health/treatments-and-wellbeing/spirituality-and-mental-health (accessed 28 April 2023).
3 J. Swinton and S. Pattison, 'Spirituality. Come all ye faithful', in *The Health Service Journal* v. 111 (20 December 2001), pp. 24–5.
4 M. Haig, *The Comfort Book* (Edinburgh; Canongate, 2021) p. 7.

1 Honesty

1 B. Brown, *Atlas of the Heart: Mapping Meaningful Connection and the Language of Human Experience* (New York: Vermilion/Penguin Random House, 2021), p. 14.
2 B. Brown, *The Gifts of Imperfection* (New York: Vermilion/Penguin Random House, 2020), p. 6.
3 L. Gottlieb, 'Lori Gottlieb: Therapist Reveals the Mindset Hacks to Completely Change Your Life!', *The Mindset Mentor with Rob Dial*: https://www.youtube.com/watch?v=xlIsDwfc7ks (23 April 2021, accessed 12 July 2023).
4 E. Eger, *The Choice* (London: Rider/Penguin Random House, 2017), p. 10.
5 C. Jung, *Memories, Dreams, Reflections: An Autobiography* (New York, NY: Vintage, 1963), p. 356.
6 Conversation between Sir Terry Waite and Patrick Regan on the Go Gently Tour, 2023.

2 Anxiety

1 K. Corley, 'Anxiety is the Most Caring Person in the Room': https://kirstencorley.wordpress.com/2020/05/20/anxiety-is-the-most-caringperson-in-the-room (20 May 2020, accessed 19 July 2022).

2 Corley, 'Anxiety is the Most Caring Person in the Room'.

3 These answers were provided via Facebook when I asked those connected with me what anxiety feels like to them.

4 C. Brotheridge, *The Anxiety Solution* (London: Penguin Random House, 2017), p. 108.

5 For more on this, see J. Oliver, 'The Unwelcome Party Guest', YouTube: https://www.youtube.com/watch?v=VYht-guymF4&ab_channel=JoeOliver (31 January 2011, accessed 19 May 2023).

6 'The Stress Bucket', Mental Health UK: https://mentalhealth-uk.org/blog/the-stress-bucket (accessed 16 May 2023).

7 Adapted from '30 Grounding Techniques to Quiet Distressing Thoughts', Healthline: https://www.healthline.com/health/grounding-techniques (accessed 20 July 2022).

8 'Serenity Prayer', attributed to Reinhold Niebuhr (1890–1971).

3 Depression

1 W. Bray and C. Ledger, *An Insight into Depression* (Surrey: Waverley Abbey Trust, 2009), p. 41.

2 T. Cantopher, *Depressive Illness: The Curse of the Strong* (London: Sheldon Press, 2003), p. 4.

3 'Suicides in England and Wales, 2021 registrations', Office for National Statistics: https://www.ons.gov.uk/peoplepopulationandcommunity/birthsdeathsandmarriages/deaths/bulletins/suicidesintheunitedkingdom/2021registrations#suicides-in-england-and-wales (accessed 17 May 2023).

4 J. Smith, 'Just one candle', used with author's permission.

5 M. Haig, *Reasons to Stay Alive* (Edinburgh: Canongate, 2016), p. 86.

6 Romans 4:18, AMP.

7 D. B. Seaburn, 'Hoping Against Hope', *Psychology Today*: https://www.psychologytoday.com/gb/blog/going-out-not-knowing/201909/hoping-against-hope (4 September 2019, accessed 1 May 2023).

8 Adapted from 'SEEKLIFT: Positive Steps to Wellbeing', Getselfhelp.co.uk: https://www.getselfhelp.co.uk/seek-lift (accessed 2 May 2023).

9 Also adapted from 'SEEK LIFT – Positive Steps to Wellbeing',

getselfhelp: https://www.youtube.com/watch?v=Hoe_k5HlPfI (1 January 2017, accessed 2 August 2022).

4 Shame

1 W. van der Hart and R. Waller, *Power of Belonging: Discovering the Confidence to Lead from Within* (Colorado Springs, CO: David C. Cook, 2019), p. 27.

2 H. Churchill and C. Musters, *Insight into Shame* (Surrey: Waverley Abbey Trust, 2019), p. 20.

3 B. Manning, 'Did you believe that I loved you?', YouTube, https://www.youtube.com/watch?v=4AehcGSIkZw (26 March 2017, accessed 2 May 2023).

4 L. R. Knost, *Two Thousand Kisses a Day: Gentle Parenting Through the Ages and Stages* (Little Hearts Books, 2013).

5 Anger

1 W. Bray and C. Ledger, *Insight into Anger* (Surrey: Waverley Abbey Trust, 2007), p. 26.

2 R. W. Firestone, 'The Simple Truth about Anger', *Psychology Today*, https://www.psychologytoday.com/gb/blog/the-human-experience/201410/the-simple-truth-about-anger (28 October 2014, accessed 31 August 2022).

3 Cited by M. Kirsch, 'Something for families to shout about', *The Times*: https://www.thetimes.co.uk/article/something-for-families-to-shout-about-3gh38j80x0b (22 April 2006, accessed 5 July 2023).

4 S. David, *Emotional Agility* (London: Penguin, 2016), chapter 7.

5 Bray and Ledger, *Insight into Anger*, p. 39.

6 T. Waite, *Out of the Silence* (London: SPCK, 2016), p. 88.

7 Perfectionism

1 Brown, *Atlas of the Heart*, p. 146.

2 Adapted from P. Regan with L. Hoeksma, *Bouncing Forwards: Notes on Resilience, Courage and Change* (Surrey: Waverley Abbey Trust, 2021), pp. 138–9.

3 Bryan Stevenson, *Just Mercy* (London: Scribe UK, 2015), p. 290.

4 K. Reivich and A. Shatté, *The Resilience Factor* (Danvers, MA: Broadway Books, 2002), p. 125.

8 Forgiveness

1 B. D. Perry and O. Winfrey, *What Happened to You? Conversations on Trauma, Resilience, and Healing* (New York: Flatiron Books, 2021), p. 219.

2 N. Colier, 'What Is Forgiveness and How Do You Do It?', *Psychology Today*: https://www.psychologytoday.com/gb/blog/inviting-monkey-tea/201803/what-is-forgiveness-and-how-do-you-do-it (15 March 2018, accessed 3 May 2023).

3 Adapted from E. L. Worthington, 'REACH Forgiveness of Others': http://www.evworthington-forgiveness.com/reach-forgiveness-of-others (accessed 14 October 2022).

4 This is still a challenge for many veterans. There is some research that suggests more US soldiers died from suicide than in battle. You can read more in this article: P. Dvorak, 'Suicide takes more military lives than combat, especially among women', *Washington Post*: www.washingtonpost.com/dc-md-va/2022/05/30/military-suicide-women-sexual-assault-ptsd (30 May 2022, accessed 3 May 2023).

5 Adapted from P. Regan, *When Faith Gets Shaken* (Oxford: Monarch Books, 2015), p. 152.

9 Self-acceptance

1 Adapted from A. Laibowitz, '12 ways to practise self-acceptance', happiness.com: www.happiness.com/magazine/personal-growth/self-acceptance (accessed 18 October 2022).

2 S. Waters, 'The path to self-acceptance, paved through daily practice': https://www.betterup.com/blog/self-acceptance (5 August 2021, accessed 26 October 2022).

3 P. Scazzero, 'Leaders, Here's One Powerful Way to Face Your Shadow': https://churchsource.com/blogs/ministry-resources/leaders-heres-one-powerful-way-to-face-your-shadow (accessed 3 May 2023).

4 Adapted from J. Earley and B. Weiss, 'The Seven Types of Inner Critics', IFS Therapy: https://personal-growth-programs.com/the-seven-types-of-inner-critics (accessed 26 October 2022).

5 You can watch Jean's story on the Kintsugi Hope YouTube channel: www.youtube.com/watch?v=5VH22NGdiiM (accessed 20 June 2023).

6 H. Nouwen, *Life of the Beloved: Spiritual Living in a Secular World* (New York, NY: Crossroad Publishing, 1962), pp. 31, 33.

10 Healthy relationships

1 M. Szalavitz, 'Touching Empathy: Lack of physical affection can actually kill babies', *Psychology Today*: https://www.psychologytoday.com/gb/blog/born-love/201003/touching-empathy (1 March 2010, accessed 15 November 2022).

2 K. Palladino, 'Mother Teresa saw loneliness as leprosy of the West', *News-Times*: https://www.newstimes.com/news/article/Mother-Teresa-sawloneliness-as-leprosy-of-the-250607.php (17 April 2004, accessed 15 November 2022).

3 'Loneliness and Mental Health', Mental Health Foundation: https://www.mentalhealth.org.uk/explore-mental-health/loneliness (accessed 17 May 2023).

4 Abridged from CDC, available on the agency website for no charge ('Loneliness and Social Isolation Linked to Serious Health Conditions', https://www.cdc.gov/aging/publications/features/lonely-older-adults.html, accessed 17 May 2023).

5 Adapted from S. Mcleod, 'Attachment Theory: Bowlby and Ainsworth's Theory Explained', Simply Psychology: https://www.simplypsychology.org/attachment.html (11 June 2023, accessed 4 May 2023).

6 C. Rogers cited in J. Smith, '"Accurate Empathy": Psychotherapy's Scalpel', American Psychiatric Association: https://psychnews.psychiatryonline.org/doi/full/10.1176/appi.pn.2021.8.37 (24 August 2021, accessed 4 July 2023).

7 H. Plett, 'What it means to "hold space" for people', Shalom House of Prayer: https://shalomcarcoar.com/2017/02/21/

what-it-means-to-hold-space-for-people-heather-plett (21 February 2017, accessed 10 November 2022).

8 B. Brown, 'Brené Brown: 3 Ways to Set Boundaries: The importance of knowing when, and how, to say no', Oprah.com: https://www.oprah.com/spirit/how-to-set-boundaries-brene-browns-advice (accessed 4 July 2023).

9 N. G. Tawwab, Instagram, https://www.instagram.com/p/B-2poMMDKtF/?hl=en (11 April 2020, accessed 27 June 2023).

10 J. Smith, 'Holding space', used with author's permission.

11 Resilience

1 C. Johnstone, *Seven Ways to Build Resilience* (London: Robinson, 2019), p. 20.

2 Johnstone, *Seven Ways to Build Resilience*, p. 47.

3 J. Collins, *Good to Great: Why Some Companies Make the Leap … and Others Don't* (New York, NY: Random House Business, 2001) p. 85.

4 Collins, *Good to Great*, p. 83.

5 V. E. Frankl, *Man's Search for Meaning* (London: Rider, 2004), p. 112.

6 J. Smith, 'without the rain', used with author's permission.